Passion:

The Life and Loves of Alexander Hamilton

Book One – The Islands

by Diane K. McCarty

ISBN: 9798710264669

Library of Congress Control Number: 2018675309

Printed in the United States of America

Dedication

This book is dedicated to Alexander Hamilton, who, with his fascinating life, urged me to write this.

A warning to parents:

This book contains frank and explicit material of a mature nature which may not be suitable to be read by minors. I have published another version, "The Library Edition," which is censored. If you wish for your children to read my book about Alexander Hamilton, I recommend you give them the censored version.

This uncensored version contains violence, profanity, and sexual themes. The "Library" version is PG-rated and contains none of the above except for a small amount of violence.

Table of Contents

A Preview of *Passion, The Life and Loves of Alexander Hamilton, Book 2*

Foreword

If you are well-versed in the lore of Alexander Hamilton's life in the West Indian islands, you will notice that I have filled in some of the gaps in our knowledge of it. For my reasons behind this, whenever you encounter something you don't agree with or wish to know why I wrote it, please read my response to the pertinent question in the Appendix at the end of this text.

Chapter One: The Mother

St. Croix, 1745

He had shown up like a lightning bolt, this "dashing" young man, this John Michael Levine. He had dazzled people acquainted with young Rachael Faucette, an heiress, daughter of Dr. Jean Faucette, deceased. Ultimately, Levine had won over Rachael's mother Mary Uppington Faucette. But could he win over the daughter?

"A fine one," said Mary. "Your brother-in-law James Lytton vouches for him. As do all our other mutual acquaintances. He is not ill-favored, is he?"

Rachael shrugged. "He is... older than me, but I reckon he is handsome enough."

"That's the spirit, dear. And he is wealthy. You saw the gold jewelry and the smart clothing, with gold buttons, no less! I'm afraid the accounts of your father's estate have shown some... depreciation of late. He did not tend to his estates sufficiently in his declining years. You will be in need of a well-to-do husband to continue to live in the manner to which you have been accustomed. Not only that, but this sugar business requires significant capital to remain competitive and succeed, as you are well aware."

"Yes, Mama."

"Unfortunately, you are under legal age. As such, you cannot inherit and control the estate until you come of age or marry. We need that money, Rachael. We need it now. I can no longer receive the alimony your father paid after we separated."

Fear crept into Rachael's heart. She had to marry someone or starve? And yet....

"But I do not know this man, much less love him."

"Love!" cried Mary. "Hah! What is love? Just a pretty flower that blooms and quickly fades, then shrivels and dies!" Was her mother speaking from her *own* experience? "An estate, financial security, that is what every young woman needs. A husband to maintain and preserve it all, to bedeck you in jewels. You may even come to love him, but if not, you will still live a fine life. Don't let such a fleeting and sentimental notion as 'love' stand in your way!"

"Could I not stay with my sister Ann for a time? She married a rich man. Just until I…'

"Don't be such a baby, Rachael! It's time you grew up. It would be rude to even ask, not only rude to Mr. Levine and his proposal, but rude to your sister who has her own life. I am certain her husband would never agree to take you in. It would be awkward in the extreme. Besides, this is a rich man and a gentleman. He would no doubt treat you well. That is all a young married lady need ask."

It seemed to make *sense* at the time, if not for the misgivings in Rachael's heart, if not for the greedy look in Levine's eyes - she hadn't just *imagined* that, had she? Despite her mother's dismissals of Rachael's concerns, she wanted to believe that he truly loved her. She wanted to believe that marriage to him would be a good thing. He spoke of his plans to own a large sugar plantation and to shower

Rachael with jewels. He *seemed* sincere. But... *did* he love her? He had said so, but....

He had wooed her. He *was* good looking at least, and *seemed* to be a rich man, bedizened with gold jewels. He had even given her a shiny gold bracelet. Perhaps, in time, she *would* come to love him. Rachael could think of no logical objection to his marriage proposal.

Therein lay her doom.

The courtship, if one could call it that, was brief. The wedding, during which she was attended by her older sisters Ann and Jemima, passed in a quick blur. Afterward, nervous, Rachael lay down to bed with Levine. She had heard that the first time was painful. And it was, a little. But she was tough, and she bore it in silence. He was not gentle, but not brutal, either. In fact, he was... somewhat detached. In like manner, his "treatment" of her continued throughout their honeymoon. Even though the pain diminished, there was never the enjoyment she had heard tell of. He simply didn't seem to care, neither about her, nor her pleasure. He would finish quickly, then withdraw in more ways than one. His interactions with her outside the bedchamber were minimal as he busied himself with spending the money she had inherited from her father. Despite the impression he'd given Rachael and her mother, Levine turned out *not* to have any money of his own. Rachael was shocked and dismayed to discover that Levine actually had been deeply *in debt* when he'd married her. Granted, he was trying to succeed in the sugar business (or, at least, so he had *told* her), like so many other hopefuls in the Caribbean islands. But he simply did not know what he was doing. Until he figured that out, the funds were inexorably being depleted. To make matters worse, he insisted on living a very extravagant lifestyle, spending liberally on domestic slaves, clothing, jewelry and other luxuries.

Sadly, Rachael concluded that she had not only committed herself to a loveless marriage, but to a penniless man at that. She should have waited. She should have stood up to her mother. She shouldn't have sold herself so cheaply. She was better than that. She *deserved* better than that.

Before long, she was with child. Perhaps she would find love as a mother. The babe, when he arrived, was constantly squalling, an endless confusion of need and mess. Rachael suffered a depression and John was no help. The baby was her problem, he'd say, and could she "just fucking shut him up?" Rachael bristled inside every time he swore at her. She had been raised in a very genteel manner and did not relish the thought of her son growing up hearing and speaking such salty language. The boy would end up fit for nothing more than an ungentlemanly occupation if this continued.

"Hush, hush, Peter," Rachael would say, over and over, rocking him. She sang him lullabies, or tried to, over the loud bawling. Nothing helped.

"I knew you'd be a shitty mother," Levine said.

"*You* try to silence him!" she said back.

He hit her across the mouth. "*Never* speak that way to me again or your son won't have a mother!" He stormed out to get drunk at a local pub.

Rachael could have cried. A weaker woman would have. But she gritted her teeth and went about her work. Rachael reckoned Levine was upset at his failures in the sugar business and he was taking it out on her. Like it or not, she was caught in his trap. She was his wife and mother to his son. She couldn't leave. *Could she?* "Contentment" was the ironic name of their cotton plantation home. Not a single member of her wretched family was the least bit content.

She stuck it out for the child's sake, so he could have both his mother and his father. She didn't want him to have a broken home like she had had herself when her parents had separated. She told herself it was the right thing to do. She had made her bed; she must now lie in it. Speaking of which, Levine would lie down next to her on those nights he wasn't obviously seeking consolation in the arms of another woman. He would often come home smelling of sex and a cheap whore's perfume. At other times, he emerged from the fields, smelling like sex and sweat. Rachael would try to ignore the shrieks and cries she heard coming from the slave quarters knowing that he was forcing himself on them whenever he got drunk. And he drank all the time.

He wouldn't touch her. He wouldn't talk to her, unless it was to complain about how she handled the child, the house, or whatever other petty complaints he could find or invent. Sometimes, he wouldn't even *look* at her for days. She didn't mind; she'd rather have him ignore her.

Years went by like this, and Rachael began to feel something new: resentment. It was growing inside of her. So many times, despite her desire not to break up the family, she had been tempted to just leave. Just take the boy and leave.

When Peter was about 3 years old, things went from indifferent to decidedly worse between his parents. Levine had had a deal go bad, *really* bad. He had sunk most of their remaining borrowed money in the venture and it went completely belly up due to his mishandling of the funds. He had to sell off his share of the plantation and they moved to Beeston Hill, a decided step down from Contentment. Levine's mood went from quiet to downright angry. He would strike out at Rachael, unprovoked, beat her, insult her, sometimes even *choke* her. He was taking his frustrations out on her. She could tell he was drinking. She would also find empty bottles of laudanum throughout the house. He had no medicinal need for it. So, he was abusing the opiate.

I don't need to live like this, Rachael told herself, and, again, she resolved to leave him. But where would she go? She didn't want to go back to her mother. Mary Faucette might even refuse to take her in and would no doubt tell her to grow up and return to her husband. Rachael had access to very little money. Levine would only give her enough to buy groceries and a few other needs. Her daily trip to the market was the only bright part of each day, the only time she could escape her abusive husband.

On one of these particular trips, she spied a man peering through a surveying instrument. He then sketched something on a piece of parchment. The man had a handsome profile, despite squinting one eye shut. Rachael forgot about her trip, her purpose, her*self*. She hadn't been aware that she had been staring until the man turned around and saw her. Suddenly, she felt very self-conscious.

He smiled at her. "Hello," he said warmly.

"Uh... hi. I'm Rachael. Rachael Levine."

"I am Johan Cronenberg, Miss Levine." He spoke with a pleasant, mild Danish accent.

"Ummm... actually, it's *Mrs.* Levine."

"My apologies, ma'am."

"You're a surveyor?"

"Ah. Yes. I've been sent here by the Danish West Indian Company to draft an up-to-date map of St. Croix."

"Really?" Rachael brightened up, stepping closer. "May I see it?"

"It's nowhere near to being finished, but you're certainly welcome."

He held the parchment, spreading it between his hands. She leaned over, looking close for a minute. It was in color, and even had little green trees all over the place. The names of the owners of the plots of land were written on the map, along with little drawings of their houses.

"That's my sister's house there!" She pointed at the plot identified as belonging to "James Lytton." "It's called 'The Grange.'"

"Nice to know," he said.

Her eyes drifted down to the right and she saw her own husband's name. The smile disappeared from her face.

He noticed. "What is wrong?"

"Nothing." She put a fake smile on her face. She straightened up and looked at him, smiling. "This is well done. I'm very impressed."

"Thank you, ma'am." He smiled, beaming at her.

"Could you show me how to use this?" She pointed to his surveying tool.

"Certainly. It's called a theodolite. You look through these slits, here and here… Close one eye when you do so." She bent slightly and looked.

"I see. And the compass at the bottom tells you the direction." she said after a few seconds of looking.

"That's right. You catch on quick!"

She shrugged. "It's pretty obvious, actually." She laughed and he joined her.

He reached over and said, "May I touch your hand?"

She nodded.

He gently took it and put it on a handle of the instrument, then moved hand and handle, shifting its position as he did so. The feeling of his hand on hers gave her a thrilling, tingling sensation that settled in her groin. It was... *stirring.*

"That's very… *interesting*," she said, breathless. "I would like to discuss it further with you, but I'm afraid I have a lot to do today. I certainly hope to see you again soon, Mr. Cronenberg."

"As do I, Mrs. Levine," he said, and smiled.

Rachael arranged it so that she could see "Cro" (as she later nicknamed him) every time she went to market. Before long, it was clear to both of them that they were not only very attracted to each other, but that they were falling in love. The first time they kissed, he touched her arm on a spot that Levine had recently injured. She winced.

"I'm sorry," he said. "I didn't intend to hurt you."

"It's okay. It's just--" She pulled back the sleeve of her blouse and exposed the bruise underneath.

"My dear lady," he said in shock. "What could have happened to you?"

"It...." She struggled not to cry, but it was a losing battle. "My husband. He... he beats me."

"Whatever for...?"

She shook her head. "He just does. When he's in his cups, you know. I'm just a convenient target."

"That's *horrible*," said Cronenberg. "I would never raise a hand to you. Any man that would do that to his wife doesn't deserve to have one."

"You're not married, are you?"

"No. But if I had such a beautiful and amiable wife as you, I would cherish her."

She smiled, but sadly. "Oh, if only I weren't married!"

"Listen, if you ever feel threatened, or you just need a place to go, to get away, I can take you in." His warm eyes were gazing at her with sympathy.

"That… that is kind of you, but it would be improper."

"Damn propriety. I see a damsel in distress, and I cannot sit back and do nothing to help her."

Rachael smiled and paused for a moment, considering. "Can I bring my little boy too?"

"Absolutely. I have slaves. They can help with the boy if need be."

She smiled and kissed him again. They continued to see each other. Cronenberg showed her tenderness and love – something she had never experienced before - but she did not give her body to him just yet, not completely.

A few weeks passed. And then one night, one *terrible* night, Levine came home drunker than usual, and that was really saying something. He stumbled into the bedroom and woke her up from a deep sleep. He pulled the covers off of her and lay on top of her, pinning her with his weight. She could smell rum and laudanum on his breath. Her heart started to pound with terror, and she tried to push him away, but he weighed too much, and he restrained her arms. "What happened?" he asked, slurring his words.

She gasped with fright. "What?"

"'*What*'?" he said, mocking her. "What happened to us! To *this!*" He began to pull up her night dress.

"Stop it!" she cried out.

"Stop? *Stop?*" He drew his hand back and slapped her, hard. "I'm your *husband,* you fucking bitch! It's your duty to submit to me. *No one* but me! Have you been giving it to someone else? Huh?"

"*NO!*" She struggled against him.

"*You lying WHORE!*" He punched her face.

She cried out in shock and pain but kept struggling. He grabbed both her wrists in one big hand. With the other, he lowered his trousers and removed his engorged manhood. She screamed, but that didn't deter him. He raped her, mercilessly. It went on and on, a nightmare she couldn't escape from, moment after interminable moment, thrust after painful thrust. After what seemed a very long time, he finally finished. He lay back next to her and fell into a stupor.

She was crying. *That's it,* she thought. *I am done with him! It's over! This man will never touch me again. I swear it!*

Chapter Two: The Lover

She moved in with Cronenberg the next morning as Levine slept off his drinking binge. She packed some clothes and took Peter with her.

At first, it was pure heaven. Rachael finally found out that the act of sexual intercourse could actually be enjoyable - *very* enjoyable. She experienced her first orgasm with Cronenberg. And then she wanted it more and more and more. Before long, she was having multiple orgasms and very intense ones at that. Her bruises were healing, as was her heart. The one thing troubling her was the thought that Levine must surely be looking for her and that it was more likely than not that he would find her. In fact, she felt it must be inevitable. She savored the time she spent with Cronenberg, wondering how long it would last.

A few months later, she knew the answer.

A slave answered the loud knock that night. In burst Levine, accompanied by three constables. They asked the slave where the master was, and she showed them the bedroom door. It was locked. They banged on the door. Rachael had been contentedly sleeping in Cronenberg's arms, both naked after a long session of lovemaking, when the loud sound awoke them.

"A moment, please!" Cronenberg cried out, putting on his breeches. He opened the door. Levine burst in, followed by the constables.

"What are you doing here?" Rachael yelled, hugging the sheet to herself.

"Arrest them!" Levine said, pointing at Cronenberg. "That's my wife he's in bed with."

"No!" Rachael could only watch, helpless.

Cronenberg struggled, but it was clearly in vain and he desisted.

Rachael began to cry. *"Cro!"*

"I'll come back to you!" he called out as two of the constables began to drag him away.

"No, you won't!" Levine told him. "She's *my* wife. You'll not touch her again, or I'll fucking kill you!" He turned to Rachael. "You're coming home with me, *wife.*" He picked up her dress, which had been discarded on the floor and threw it on top of her. "Get dressed." He looked to the remaining constable. "Wait outside."

The man exited, closing the door.

Red-faced, Rachael got out of bed and began to put the dress on as Levine watched, an annoyingly smug look on his face. "You will be a dutiful wife to me. You will turn from your evil ways and come home with me."

She held back tears with an iron will. "Is it my duty to submit to your ravishments?"

"Shut up!" Then he slapped her.

She looked at him with anger but held her tongue. She decided to feign compliance - for now.

Levine asked a slave where the little boy was. He picked Peter up and carried him out. The constable followed and pulled

Rachael all the way home. He left her with Levine, who beat her senseless.

"Tomorrow, you are going to bathe that man off of you. I will not touch you with his... *juices* covering you. Then you are going to be a proper wife to me. For the rest of your life." He tied her to the bed with a smelly old hemp rope. He fell asleep next to her. She was up all night, frightened and quietly crying.

Rachael struggled to free herself from the rope, chewing through it like an animal while Levine was gone during the day. She made slow progress, which she hid from Levine whenever he was around. *This is what he has reduced me to!* she thought, bitterly. She refused to bathe herself, so Levine wouldn't touch her. Finally, in frustration, he had a slave do it while he went out drinking and God knows what else. That night, she was finally able to free herself. She took Peter and sneaked out of the house, heading straight for Cronenberg's home. He was there and took her in his arms, gently because of the bruises and cuts, which were visible everywhere, including her face.

"Oh, my darling! I was so afraid of what Levine would--"

"Shh, shh. I'll be okay. I'll heal. What happened to you?"

"Nothing much. They threw me in a cell for a few days. I just got out tonight. I was going to check on you tomorrow. There is one thing you should know: they released me with the injunction that I should never see you again."

"Oh! That's horrible! What are you going to do?"

"Ignore them and keep you with me."

"But what if they arrest you?"

"I don't care. I love you. Let them arrest me. That won't stop me loving you."

"But Levine knows where we are. He'll come here."

"We'll find an inn to stay at tonight. Tomorrow, I'll rent a house. We'll pack some things and go. *Now.*"

She smiled and nodded.

They passed the summer together, pleasuring each other as much as possible. When not so occupied, Cronenberg continued to progress in his drafting of the map. He had to move about from place to place; of course, Rachael and Peter went with him.

Free of Levine, Rachael had the opportunity to bond with Peter without worrying about being interrupted by her husband's bullying of her. If only she and Cronenberg could have been married, things would have been *perfect.* Alas, it was not to be. Time was passing. If only she could stop it and stay with "Cro" forever.

It was a warm October evening in their tropical paradise. Rachael and Cronenberg were engaged in another blissful marathon session of lovemaking. Cronenberg was thrusting all the way inside of her. She threw her head back, eyes closed, crying out with ecstasy as the orgasm exploded within her.

"STOP!" shouted a horrible voice. One she knew all too well. *Levine.*

She opened her eyes, horrified. Cronenberg was pulled out of her and off of her, by Levine and a constable. It was too much to bear.

Embarrassed by her nudity, Rachael pulled a sheet over herself. Levine had found them, and the awful nightmare was repeating itself. But this time, it would last much, much longer.

They were both arrested, dragged to the dungeon prison at Fort Christiansvaern and locked in separate cells. Two days later, they were brought to trial. Levine and the constables were present to testify. The charge: having twice committed adultery. The verdict was no surprise: *guilty*.

The days stretched out into timeless ennui. She thought of Cronenberg and the love they had shared. She thought of the pleasure he had given her. She *ached* for him. She cried. It was so unfair. She had finally found happiness and now *this?* She missed her son and dreaded what Levine might do to him now that he could no longer take his frustrations out on her. Did he beat *Peter* now? Her fears for her son were agonizing.

She was confined to a dank little cell, with nothing but a tiny window to look out of. She was fed nothing much but salted fish and tasteless corn mush. She barely ate it and started to lose weight. Not that she had much to lose.

Levine visited her once. Just once. It was about a month into her incarceration. She looked daggers at him.

"I've decided I don't want you to stay here any longer," he said. "Come home to me. Be my wife. Be Peter's mother. We'll start again, do better this time. You, my dutiful wife, will do all that I tell you to do. That's my condition. You will submit to me and stop committing adultery."

"You hypocrite! How many women, how many *whores* have you slept with since being married to me? How many slaves have you forced yourself upon? I only left you for another man because you *raped* me!"

"A husband cannot rape his wife. You married me willingly and must willingly do your wifely duty to me. I would have more sons from you."

"Never!" she cried out.

His face flushed red with anger. "You'll change your tune 'ere long. A few months of isolation should do it. You'll be begging to be released before it's over. Just remember, you brought this on yourself with your whoring ways."

"I am *not* a whore!" she yelled to his back as he was leaving.

Time creeped slowly on during the rest of her imprisonment. To occupy her restless mind in those endless months, weeks, days, hours, minutes, and seconds; she devised exquisite methods of torture and vengeance to exact on the man who had so wronged her, playing and re-playing the execution of them in her mind with relish. The longer she was imprisoned, the more elaborate these schemes grew, until they became somewhat anatomically impossible. The torture instruments of her imaginings became more and more infeasible. Still, what gave her her only pleasure was picturing Levine's face twisted in paroxysms of pain; his bones contorted, broken, splintered. In her fantasies, his sexual organs were so horribly tortured and maimed that he begged for their amputation.... A conscientious thought occurred to her: *What is he turning me into?* She brushed the pesky thought aside.

She wrote to her mother, telling her of the deplorable conditions she was being subjected to and begging her to come and bring some books for her to read to occupy her time. Her mother complied. She began to cry when she saw what her daughter had been reduced to.

"Why did you do it?" Mary asked. "Why did you leave him for the arms of another man?"

Rachael told her about Levine's many cruelties, up to and including the rape. That brought fresh tears to her mother's eyes that rolled down her flushed cheeks.

"I feel so guilty," Mary said. "I blame myself. I made you marry him."

"I'll forgive you, Mama, if you help me get out of here."

"I will do what I can. I can't promise it will be any time soon. Oh, my poor baby!"

Finally, when she thought she'd at

last go mad with boredom, the books notwithstanding, Rachael was released. It had been almost seven months. Seven long, terrible months. Nevertheless, even prison was preferable to living with Levine. He was standing outside the prison, waiting for her with her mother. They totally ignored each other.

"Are you ready to resume your rightful place at my side, *wife?*" Levine asked, as Rachael stepped outside.

She glared at him. "There is one thing and *only* one thing I want from you."

"And what is that?"

"My son."

"He's home. Come with me if you want him."

Rachael looked at her mother, giving her a slightly pleading look. She wanted to go with Levine, but not alone. Mary understood.

Levine entered a waiting coach. Rachael and Mary entered another, and they all headed for the Levine house.

When they arrived there, as soon as the women stepped out of their coach, Levine told Mary, "I would speak with my wife alone, first."

She looked at Rachael who nodded. She followed her husband into the house. Peter was there with a servant; Rachael dropped to one knee as he ran into her arms.

"I missed you, Mama!" Peter said.

"Oh, my darling boy," Rachael said. "I've missed you too." She kissed him and whispered in his ear, "Does he beat you?"

Much to her relief, the boy shook his head.

The servant said, "If there is anything you'll be needing from me, Mr. Levine…"

"Just one more thing. I want you and my son to witness something. That being, how a wife is supposed to *treat* her husband." He looked at Peter. "Step away from your mother."

"But—"

"Now," Levine said in a tone that would not tolerate disobedience.

Rachael stood up as Peter moved away. Her heart beat rapidly, filled with a sense of foreboding.

"Get back down on your knees," he told her.

She frowned. "Why?"

"Do you want to continue to see your son?"

"Yes."

"Then do it."

She hesitated. "I…" She turned to Peter; their eyes locked. She didn't want him to see a woman being treated like this. She didn't want him to grow up to be like his father. Most of all, she wanted Peter to know that this man could be defied so that when the time came, he could do so as well.

"No."

Frustrated, Levine pushed her down on her knees. Shaking, she glared up at him.

"Loosen my fly, pull it out, and suck it."

"Never." The unmitigated *gall* of the man, to demand such an indecent act, and in front of their own son!

He slapped her. She recoiled, recovered, and stood up. He raised a fist to hit her, but she blocked the blow and spat in his face.

He wiped the spittle off, then said, "Very well then, if that is your choice…." He reached into his jacket pocket and pulled out a piece of paper. "Read this."

With trepidation, Rachael took the document. It was a court order. She was shocked at what she read, and tears suffused her eyes, but she held them in check. She would never let him see her cry, no matter what. She let anger fill her, red and burning. Levine had had her declared an unfit mother and had received full custody of Peter. Levine now had the right to forbid her visitation with the boy.

"I will give you one last chance to change your mind, my dear," he said, smugly and without the slightest trace of affection for her, despite referring to her with a term of endearment. "You can stay here with me, be my *dutiful* wife and do absolutely everything I say. All will be forgiven… *after* you have performed the proper… *penance.*" His voice savored the word. She knew full well what he had in mind and she felt nauseous just at the thought of it. "Or… you can leave and never return. And you will *never, ever* see *my* son again."

Rachael closed her eyes and began to think. She loved her son more than life itself. She would go through fire, through hell and any kind pain for him. But she would not, *could not* live with that man. Furthermore, she could not allow her son – *her* son! – to grow up watching his father abuse his mother and be corrupted by it. She would rather die. She would retreat and see what she could do to overturn the travesty of justice written on that paper she had just read.

Someday, perhaps, an opportunity would come for her to regain custody of her son. For now, she had no choice but to walk away even though she felt her heart tearing apart at the seams.

She summoned her rage and faced Levine. "I love *my* son more than you ever will. You have no heart. Only a monster would tear a child away from his mother! I curse you, Levine. You will die someday. You will die alone and penniless. And then, you will go to Hell."

She turned to face Peter. "I love you, Peter. I will love you forever. Be a good man. Don't be like… *him*."

"I will, Mama!"

Levine's face flushed with anger. He grabbed her arm. "How dare you speak this way about me in front of my son!"

She shrugged his hand off. "I will speak about you and to you in whatever manner I *choose*. You are not the boss of me." Then, she said a word that her genteel upbringing had strictly forbade her to ever say, though she had heard Levine use this most vulgar of words many times. "You can go *fuck* yourself, Levine, for I never shall again!"

Holding her head high, she stepped toward the door. Levine was so stunned, he just stood there, speechless, and did not try to stop her from leaving. Rachael departed in the coach with her mother and never looked back. She smiled. It had felt good to use that word and to so defy the scumbag she had married. Still, it was a sad smile. She had paid a high price for her defiance. She very well might never see Peter again. *Oh, God,* she prayed, *watch over my son. Bring him safely back to me.*

Rachael and her mother left St. Croix for the island of St. Christopher, which was often called "St. Kitts." She made some inquiries and found out that Cronenberg had been sentenced to exile. He had fought the adultery charge and its punishment in court but had failed. He could never see her again. Rachael grieved for him, but she could do nothing. It was over. She must move on.

Curse Levine! Must he take everyone I love away from me?

Chapter Three: The Father

"Your shirt needs repair, Red," Rachael said, sporting that half-smile that men found so irresistible.

"I beg your pardon, Miss... " The ginger haired man spoke with a pleasant Scottish burr.

"Faucette. Rachael Faucette." She held out her hand. The man knew his manners.

He took it and, genteelly, held it up, bowing over it. Then he looked up. "And I, my dear lassie, am known as Mr. James Hamilton."

"Well, Mr. James Hamilton, give me your shirt and I'll mend it for a fair price."

"Here?"

She laughed and shook her head. "Follow me." She headed toward her shop and he followed. "It's a long way from Scotland, Mr. James Hamilton. What brings you to St. Kitts?"

"White gold, o' course. I've come to make my fortune. As the fourth son of a laird, I inherit nothing."

"Ah... so you have noble blood," she said, her tone speculative.

"Aye." Pride flashed in his blue eyes. "As soon as I have a successful sugar plantation established here, I intend to return home." His tone was somewhat wistful when he said the word "home."

"Tell me about it."

He spoke at some length of his beautiful home, a place called Kerelaw Castle in the territory his family owned named The Grange. "It overlooks a lovely glen and stream on one side, the sea and a little town on the other. On a clear day, you can see an island across the firth."

"That sounds lovely. My sister and her husband live in a lovely estate on St. Croix, also called The Grange. Not quite as grand as the home you describe, but quite fine for here in the islands. Here's my shop," said Rachael, unlocking the door. Once inside, they looked at each other for a long moment during which neither one of them said anything. "Well," said Rachael, "take it off. Don't be modest. I'm no blushing maiden."

Staring into her eyes, he stripped the shirt off. He wore an undershirt, and it was drenched with sweat. She could see his nipples through it and a moderate amount of ginger hair underneath.

Taking the shirt, she waved him to a simple wooden chair then proceeded to stitch the rent in the shirt. They spoke of their families. Every now and then, she glanced up and Hamilton started to look forward to those moments when their eyes locked. Her eyes were riveting, gray-blue on the outer part of the iris, each with a greenish starburst near to the pupil. They shone and flashed whenever she smiled. He found himself spellbound by those eyes.

Finally finished, she quoted a price. He didn't even consider if it was reasonable. He just started counting out the money. Their hands met as she handed him the shirt and he placed the money in her other palm.

"Come again, Red, if you have any more rips..." she said and gave him a brilliant smile.

'I will, lassie," he said with a wink. "Aye, and you can count on that."

She laughed and blushed.

The next day, James Hamilton showed up at Rachael's door again. "I tore muh breeches," he said.

"So I see," she said, her eyes flashing with mirth. "Take them off, Red," she said, unable to keep a slightly seductive tone from her voice.

"With pleasure, lass," he said.

Taking the pants, she gave him a piece of fabric to cover himself with; he wrapped it around his waist.

She smiled. He watched her in mostly silence. She gave him the occasional glance again, always smiling. Light danced in her eyes. Once again, they made the exchange of money for clothing, but when their hands met, they didn't let go. Their eyes locked, and nonverbal inquiries passed between them. An offer? An acceptance?

Rachael leaned in. "Is there anything else you desire, Red?"

"Aye, lass. There is. And, please, call me James."

"James..." she whispered.

Their lips met. Then, inexplicably (to James), Rachael pulled away.

"I'm sorry, lass. Have I done something wrong?"

"No, it's just that I...." Tears filled her eyes. "I'm sorry. I shouldn't do this. I care for you, but I... I'm..." She breathed in deeply and sighed, steeling herself. "I'm married," she whispered.

"Married?" James repeated. His heart sank. "Did I hear ye right? Didja just say you're married?"

She nodded, blushing. She explained how her husband had abused her and she had left him. She didn't share the gory details.

James frowned. "Would he come

after you? To get ye back?"

She shook her head. "No. It's over."

"You could try for a divorce…?"

She shrugged. "They are difficult to obtain. I could try, I suppose." She looked down, hopelessly.

"Dinna fash, lass," Hamilton said, putting a couple of fingers under her chin and lifting her head up. "A lovely young lady such as yourself. Surely, there are good things in your future."

"You think so?" she asked, her eyes hopeful.

He nodded. "There are. If I have anything to do with it. Aw, now, there's your lovely smile. If there's anything I can do to help you, I will."

"You will?" She hugged him.

"O' course I will." He loved how she felt in his arms, like she belonged there. "Dinna despair. We'll sort it all out. You'll see."

"Thank you." She kissed him on the

cheek. "Thank you so much."

"My pleasure, lass. My pleasure."

Several months down the road, after multiple inquiries of any attorney they could find, the situation only looked more and more hopeless. James did his best to keep Rachael's spirits up. He could be very amusing, as well as tender and romantic. But, ultimately, Rachael could find no legal remedy. She began to despair. If she lost James, she would lose everything that mattered to her. She was in love with him, and that love already ran even deeper than it had with Cronenberg. Cro had been sweet and sexy, and James was that, too, but he did what Cro never could – he made her laugh. She needed that in her life. She needed him. But she loved him enough that she couldn't ask him to take on her sin, to commit adultery with her, even though she wanted him in her bed so much that it was driving her insane. They had not yet consummated their relationship. She wanted to do it properly this time. But now it was looking like they wouldn't do it at all. She was starting to sink into a well of despair.

James knew all of this. She didn't have to tell him. He could see it all in her expressive eyes. He had to *do* something.

He went to the local church and explained the situation to the pastor.

The pastor said, "A wife should be with her husband."

"But her husband has been abusing her."

The man shook his head. "That is unfortunate. But—"

Desperate, James said, "He raped her!"

The reverend looked at him, shock on his face.

"He cheated on her, broke their covenant, spent all of her inheritance money on whores and loose women. When it was all gone, he returned to her and forced himself on her, against her will. She fled to the protection of another man and her husband threw her in prison for it. And then, when she got out, he wanted her to…" James paused, shaking his head. "He wanted her to commit unspeakable acts on him. Right in front of their own son! Father, please! Has God no mercy?"

The pastor looked at him with new understanding dawning in his eyes. "I… very well, I will pray on this matter and ask God. We will abide by His Will."

"Thank you, Father."

"Return tomorrow evening and I will give you the answer."

When James returned the following evening, the pastor informed him that he had prayed on the matter and felt that God was agreeable to the new marriage.

"Oh, thank you, Father!" said James, ecstatic.

"However, if I do this for you, I have conditions."

"Aye, Father. Anything."

"First of all, no one must ever know that it was done here or that I was the one to do it. Not even your relatives. No guests, no witnesses. Needless to say, it will not be entered in the church's wedding register."

"Agreed."

"Secondly, Mrs. Levine must make a full confession and beg the Lord to annul her current marriage."

Hamilton nodded.

"And lastly, this must be done at night, for secrecy. Tomorrow night, in fact, is the only time I can do this any time in the foreseeable future."

Hamilton held out his hand. The pastor took it. "I agree. Thank you, most kindly, Father. I'll bring my bride with me tomorrow night." *My bride!* he thought, excitedly.

"God bless you, my son."

"Rachael, Rachael, Rachael!" He

embraced her and lifted her off the floor, spinning her around. "I have it, lass! We can be married!"

"What? How?"

He explained the situation to her and the deal he had worked out with the pastor.

"And he said he would do this? Truly?"

"Aye!" He kissed her. "At last, we'll be married. Tomorrow night. Maybe not in the eyes of the law, but in the eyes of God. And do His eyes not count for more than the law?"

Rachael smiled. "Yes!" She kissed him, deeply. "Oh, yes. Red, this is wonderful! It's the most amazing gift anyone has ever given me."

"The first of many, I hope. In the meantime, I'll have to get you a ring. Nothing too dear, as I'm a little short on funds at the moment, but I should have enough to suffice."

"I care not for fancy rings. A simple one is fine. All I care about is you, Red." They kissed again. "I can't believe this!

We're getting married!"

"Believe it, lass. It's happening."

Hamilton introduced Rachael to the pastor. He spoke with her about why she had left her husband.

"My child," said the pastor, "I understand. I believe that God understands, as well. He did say, through his servant St. Paul, that wives should obey and submit to their husbands. But He also said that husbands should love their wives. It is clear that your husband has violated God's wishes. God does not wish for any of His children to subject themselves to the kind of abuse your husband has inflicted upon you. Furthermore, your husband was the first to commit adultery, and many times over. He was the one who broke your covenant. God does grant annulments based on such a thing."

Rachael nodded.

"I will now ask you a series of questions. Do you admit that you erred in your marriage vow?"

"I do."

"Do you ask the Lord's forgiveness for what you have done and what you are about to do?"

"I do."

"Do you submit yourself to the Lord's will?"

"I do."

"Do you reject Satan and all his evils?"

"I do."

"Do you agree to repent and sin no more?"

"I do."

"The Lord God who loves you forgives you. The Lord frees you from your sin and from the evil of the marriage you have made in error."

Tears of gratitude fell from Rachael's eyes. "Thank the Lord. Thank you, Father."

The pastor nodded, smiling. "Now, let us join the two of you in the bonds of

Holy Matrimony."

Rachael was shaking with excitement as she joined hands with James. The pastor said a few words on marriage. The words reached her heart and made it glow with love.

James asked the pastor if he could read from St. Paul's 1st Letter to the Corinthians and the man agreed. James had brought his own bible for the occasion. In his smooth Scottish burr, he read the following out loud, while occasionally pausing to look lovingly into his bride's eyes:

> *Though I speak with the tongues of men and of angels, and have not love, I am become as sounding brass, or a tinkling cymbal. And though I have the gift of prophecy, and understand all mysteries, and all knowledge; and though I have all faith, so that I could remove mountains, and have not love, I am nothing. And though I bestow all my goods to feed the poor, and have not love, it profiteth me nothing. Love*

suffereth long, and is kind; Love envieth not; Love vaunteth not itself, is not puffed up, thinketh no evil; rejoiceth not in iniquity, but rejoiceth in the truth; beareth all things, believeth all things, hopeth all things, endureth all things. Love never faileth. When I was a child, I spake as a child, I understood as a child, I thought as a child: but when I became a man, I put away childish things. For now we see through a glass, darkly; but then face to face. And now abideth faith, hope, love, these three; but the greatest of these is love.

The pastor asked them then to join hands for the following vows: "James Hamilton, wilt thou have this woman to be thy wedded wife, to live together after God's ordinance in the Holy Estate of matrimony? Wilt thou love her? Comfort her, honor and keep her, in sickness and in health, and, forsaking all others, keep thee only unto her as long as you both shall live?"

"I will," said James.

Rachael began to cry tears of joy at this. The pastor repeated the vows for her, and she, too, said, "I will."

"Then, by the power vested in me by Our Lord God, and by the Church of England, I pronounce you husband and wife. You may kiss your bride."

It was the happiest moment of their lives. They were married. Truly. Secretly, yes, but also in the most important way. The eyes of the law be damned! Levine be damned! Rachael was Mrs. Hamilton. And there was nothing else she'd rather be. And no one else she'd rather be with. "You're stuck with me now, lass," Hamilton said, smiling.

"Likewise, Red," Rachael replied.

They headed home quickly, holding hands, laughing and joking. Neither had ever been happier. James leaned her up against a tree and kissed her deeply. "Ah… what I'm going to do to you when we get home."

"If you keep kissing me like that, we're not going to make it back there…."

"Would that be such a bad thing…?"

Rachael laughed. She pushed him away teasingly and ran for the small house they were renting. He chased her and was surprised at how quickly she could run. "Dinna wear me out too much, lass!"

They were almost home. Rachael stopped and turned. "Why?" she asked with feigned innocence.

He took her in his arms. "You know why…" he said suggestively, panting, and not just from the exertion. "I must save my strength."

"For what?" Rachael asked, smiling.

He shrugged. "I dinna know. Nothin' in particular."

She laughed, as did he.

"But seriously…" Now there was a fire in his eyes as he leaned in toward her, staring deeply into hers. He said, with strong desire in his voice, "I intend to make you mine tonight. Heart… soul… and *body*. I am going to spend this entire night doing just that, until all the wee little birds start to sing the sun up…" He kissed her again and she took his hand, pulling him into the house.

They tumbled in the bed together, laughing, kissing touching. James quickly helped his wife (his *wife!)* out of her clothing. She lay back on the bed, naked, writhing seductively, with feline grace. If she could, she would have been purring. James watched her, admiring the view and not hiding it from his face. "By God, you are beautiful." He gasped, watching her, feeling himself grow uncomfortably hard. "Even more so than I imagined." He loosened his fly, peeled off his jacket, cravat, and shirt, letting them fall to the floor, not caring. He quickly removed the rest.

Rachael was surprised to see how big James was. At least an inch or two longer than her previous bedmates. She stared and gasped appreciatively; this admiration was not lost on James. He had not had a lot of partners, but those he'd been with before had had similar reactions. Rachael spread her legs enticingly.

He crawled between her legs and kissed her. "Do you want me to dive right in, lassie, or explore your body first?"

"We've been waiting more than long

enough. We can explore each other later."

He lowered himself on top of her. He pushed back his foreskin, positioned himself and began to push in. They both gasped with pleasure as he entered her. Rachael had her first orgasm of the evening within seconds and James had to hold back his own with an iron will. He wanted to make this last as long as possible. Neither of them had made love like this before. It was a revelation. It was like they had both been virgins before and were just now discovering what love truly was and what the highest possible expression of it was like when shared between a man and a woman. What they had done with others before was just for play. Oh, some of it had been very enjoyable, but none of it had been so very full of love. Their hearts were melting and melding together, becoming one. Somehow, they could each feel what the other one was feeling, and that was the purest, strongest love, beyond anything they had ever thought possible.

It went on and on. They seemed to exist outside of time. Every breath, every movement, every sound, every second was golden and long. Neither one wanted to stop. It went on for hours but felt timeless. Rachael peaked again and again, rising higher and higher. James continued to hold back, but after a time, control started to slip away from him. When he could hold back no longer, he exploded, crying out with the most intense ecstasy he had ever felt. He was in the clouds, with the brightest, purest light all around him. He and Rachael had found Heaven together. They stayed there, holding each other, until gradually and slowly descending back to Earth.

"Wow," said James, after catching his breath. "What was that?"

Rachael laughed. "The best ever."

He kissed her. "So far…"

"Mmmmm…" she said. "Are you saying we'll have it even better next time?"

"I'll do my darnedest to, lassie."

"If anyone can, you can."

"You better believe it."

"I do."

"Mm-hmm."

He kissed her, slowly and deeply, for a long time. He explored her body with his hands, his lips, his tongue. She returned the favor. There was no part of their bodies left untouched, unloved, unsatisfied. James brought her back to the heights of ecstasy many times. Sometime during that night, he found himself ready and able to enter her again, and they happily continued their blissful dance of love. True to his word, James made love to her all night long.

And they were just getting started. This was what the poets spoke of; this was the most intense lovemaking and Rachael wanted more of it. Fortunately, James had an abundance of it to share with her.

As expected, Rachael soon became pregnant. She gave birth to a girl the next year, whom they named Marie. Two years later, she had a boy. They named him James, Jr. and called him "Jemmie." After the birth of the two, they had to move to the island of St. Eustatius.

She had some difficulties after that; a child, sadly, was stillborn. Following this, she had a miscarriage after a few months of pregnancy. Fortunately, however, things did not end there and Rachael, once again, became pregnant in 1756.

Sadly, she lost her mother that year, as well. At the funeral, she reconnected with some family she had lost touch with, including her older sister Jemima Gurley. An inheritance passed to Rachael which included some real property and three slaves, all adult female domestic servants, named Rebecca, Flora and Esther. Mary had been hiring them out to Archibald Hamm for a little extra money; Rachael and James continued this arrangement. He had always treated them relatively well, and it was important to the Hamiltons that the women were not abused. They certainly did not bar the women from sexual activities if they chose to take lovers, as long as said activities were consensual. They would not abide the raping of their slaves. Hamm gave them access to male slaves. In time, the women started to give birth, which added to the household.

Rachael didn't mind attending to the household duties herself. She hadn't had to do it very much in her childhood, but she knew how to cook and clean well enough. Her mother had been quite aware of the vagaries of fortunes won and lost in the sugar trade and had seen to it that Rachael knew everything about running a household, including how to do the chores. Likewise, Rachael began to teach the same skills to Marie as soon as the girl was old enough to start learning.

Rachael was almost to full term in her pregnancy as 1756 was coming to an end. She invited her sister Jemima Gurley and her family to visit for the holidays. Older than Rachael, she had some more mature children with her. They and other relatives helped the Hamiltons move to Nevis. Rachael had inherited a property in Charlestown, the capital of Nevis. There, on January 11, 1757, a second son was born. This one they named after his grandfather, Laird of The Grange in Scotland.

Alexander Hamilton.

Chapter Four: The Prodigy

Little Alex proved to be possessed of an intelligence that in due course began to outstrip even that of his elder siblings. He had a voracious appetite for knowledge and was constantly asking questions. As soon as he could talk, he did so, almost incessantly. If Rachael hadn't loved him so much, she would have been quite annoyed by it all. His hair was a golden ginger, and his eyes were a violet-blue, like cornflowers.

Part of her dotage on Alex could, perhaps, be attributed to the fact that she knew he would be her last child. After Alexander, Rachael had gotten pregnant one last time. The pregnancy had ended in a terrible miscarriage that had nearly claimed Rachael's life and rendered her infertile. After her recovery, she spent as much time as she could with her youngest child but did not neglect the needs of the others.

James did seem to be put off a bit by Alex's insatiable curiosity, but his gentlemanly manners made him bear it politely. At every opportunity, the Hamiltons taught their children to behave in the manner of the rich and noble families they had come from, despite the fact that their fortunes had become somewhat diminished.

James had learned many maxims that he shared with his children, such as: "Good manners cost you nothing; the lack of good manners costs you everything."

Despite their occasional financial difficulties, Rachael started to find that contentment she had always longed for but had never known before. Even her all-too-brief happiness with Cronenberg had been marred by the constant trepidation of being found by Levine. Now, however, it was clear that Levine was out of the picture and she could relax and enjoy her life.

She loved her family. James was the true husband of her heart. She adored her children, and, though part of her would always miss her first son Peter, she at least found some consolation in her children with James. Marie was a pure angel, all sweetness and smiles. Jemmie was generous, handy and helpful. Even though he was never asked to, he liked to assist in repairing things around the house. He had a particular aptitude for woodworking and carpentry. Alexander, conversely, seemed more of a talker and a thinker. Collectively, the three youths were endowed with the gifts of the Heart, Body, and Mind. And she was so very proud of all of them. In James' eyes, she could see that same pride showing through whenever he looked at them.

One Sunday evening, Rachael was sitting and relaxing by reading a book of classical Roman mythology. She would read these stories to the children often at bedtime and Alex, especially, seemed to soak up the stories.

He snuggled up next to her. She put an arm around his shoulders, squeezed gently and kissed his cheek. "Can you teach me how to read like you do, Maman?" he asked.

The question surprised her. "I had planned on doing so or possibly having you tutored when you are older, mon fils," she said.

"Oui, Maman," said Alex. From the cradle, Rachael had made it a point to speak both French and English to her children. She had learned the language from her Huguenot father. Alex seemed particularly adept at learning both languages. The others knew a little French, but rarely spoke it and still called her the English "Mama." Only Alex called her the French "Maman." "Can you teach me now? I promise I'll study hard."

She laughed. "I know you will. Very well. I will teach you. Go fetch some paper and a pencil and I will start to teach you your letters first."

"Letters?"

"Combined together, they form words. Words are put together to make sentences and so on. I will teach you what all of this means, but we have to start with you learning your letters."

"I will learn my letters then. I will be the best person in the world at letters. You will see."

She laughed again, with delight. "I'm sure I will, my smart, smart boy. *Certainement.*"

Smiling, Alex ran to fetch the materials he needed.

"The boy needs a tutor!" said Rachael.

"I know, but that costs money," said James.

"I can't keep up with him! His appetite for knowledge is not just excessive, it's downright insatiable! I've made some inquiries. There's a Jewish teacher who comes highly recommended. She runs a school."

"How much will she charge?"

"I know it may be difficult at times, but Alex is worth it, and more. I negotiated a fair price with her." She told him how much.

James shrugged. "If we can afford it...." Although their present financial situation was relatively stable, James was often struggling to support the family. They had tried to run a plantation Rachael had inherited but James had not been attentive enough to it. Productivity had greatly diminished until the plantation could no longer produce enough revenue to pay its bills. They'd been forced to sell it to pay off the creditors. James' family connections helped him to find gainful employment but could only go so far. At times, James would refuse to work a job he considered beneath him and his heritage. At least they still had some slaves they could hire out for a fairly reliable, albeit small, income.

Rachael kissed him on the cheek. "I'm sure we'll manage. Our son is truly gifted. He needs a better education to reach his full potential."

"Lo tir'tsahh.... " Little Alex Hamilton was in the middle of reciting the Ten Commandments in Hebrew and English. He was the youngest and smallest in the class. Before he had begun his recitation of The Decalogue, his teacher had picked him up and stood him on top of her desk. He was smiling, comfortable to be thus elevated. "Thou shalt not murder." The teacher nodded. "Lo tin'aph... Thou shalt not commit adultery...."

Alexander wondered what adultery was. "Something adults do sometimes that they should not do," was all he was ever told. Little did he know at the time, so innocent was he, the impact that very act had had and would later have on his life.

Meanwhile, the other, older students were staring daggers at the little prodigy, jealous of his superior intelligence. Once he'd completed running through the list, his teacher applauded, which forced the children to also clap, somewhat less enthusiastically.

After a few months of the commencement of his youngest son's tutoring, James' business dealings were not panning out as well as he'd hoped. They had to stop taking Alex to the school because they couldn't afford it anymore. His mother continued to do her best to teach him on her own. She taught Marie and Jemmie as well, but she always gave Alex extra assignments.

"What are you going to be that you need to know so much, Alex?" Marie asked him.

He shrugged. "I don't know yet. Maybe I'll be a writer and people will read my books. Or a poet like Alexander Pope.

Or I'll be… I don't know… *rich.*   And I'll handle people's money or some such thing."

Marie laughed. "You have such notions, Alex. I just want to be a pretty wife and mother, like Mama."

"Marry a rich man, then." He whispered, "Not like Papa."

"But Papa is nice," she whispered back.

"Yes, well, marry a nice, rich man."

Marie laughed. "Will you be a nice, rich man?"

"I hope to be. But you can't marry me; I'm your brother."

Marie laughed and pushed her brother's shoulder teasingly. "I didn't mean I'd have to marry you, silly! Just because you're going to be rich and nice!"

Alex pushed back, gently and laughed. Soon, they were tickling each other and giggling uproariously.

Distracted, James looked up from the newspaper he had been reading. "That's enough, children," he said. "Behave like ladies and gentlemen."

They stopped their play. "Yes Papa," they said. Marie went to sit at the harpsichord her mother had inherited and began to play, as Rachael had taught her. Alex sat on her left side and smiled, watching her play. He took over the bass part. Jemmie was whittling some sticks to make a toy out of.

Rachael smiled. She had to admit, despite their financial woes, at times, their life was good. She didn't mind so much having to teach her own children. She enjoyed watching Alex's brain developing and growing. It was a wonder to behold. And then, she thought of something.

"Let me teach you a song," she said. She waved the two children apart and sat between them. "It is called 'The Nut-Brown Maid.' It's a duet between a knight and a young baron's daughter who loves him, no matter what." She began to sing the song and to play it on the harpsichord.

> *… I am the Knight, I come by night*
> *As secret as I can*
> *Saying Alas! Thus standeth the case*

I am a banished man.

She sang the knight's part in a voice so low it made the children laugh. Jemmie looked up from his work briefly and chuckled. James watched and listened to his wife, an adoring smile on his face. He stood up and headed over to the instrument, looking over her shoulder.

> *… they love true and continue:*
> *Record the Nut-brown Maid,*
> *Which, when her love came her to prove*
> *Would not depart; for in her heart*
> *She loved but him alone….*

James interrupted Rachael's singing of the man's part and started to sing it himself. She smiled, letting him do so. They continued the duet.

> *It standeth so: a deed is do*
> *Whereof great harm shall grow:*
> *My destiny is for to die*
> *A shameful death, I trow;*
> *Or else to flee. The t' one must be.*
> *None other way I know*
> *But to withdraw as an outlaw,*

And take me to my bow.
Wherefore adieu, mine own heart true!
None other rede I can:
For I must to the green-wood go,
Alone, a banished man.

The ballad went on to tell the story of how the maid wanted to go to the woods with him and he asked her question after question to test her love, loyalty, and resolve to be with him, no matter what. Would she change her appearance to a masculine one and wield a bow and arrow? Would she endure ridicule from others? Would she give up all the luxuries she was used to, living outside, exposed to the elements? Would she hunt for what little food they would have to eat? She always answered yes, for she loved only him. Finally, he asked her what she would do if he fell in love with another woman? She said that she would serve the woman but would still love him. He then revealed that he was the son of an earl and not, in fact, a banished outlaw, and that he would take her to his domain and marry her.

Alex's mind whirled as he listened to

the story unfold. He was amazed at how strong this woman's love was, that she would give up everything for this man, who was pretending to be a lowly criminal. Did such a woman exist, other than, perhaps, Maman? If so, she was the kind of woman he would want to marry someday. He would make it a quest of his that, later in life, he would find her. He would not settle for less.

In time, Marie and Alex learned the parts of the duet and began to sing them together, accompanied by their mother, at first, until they also learned to play the song together on the harpsichord.

As the Hamilton children were growing, the children of their parents' slaves were as well. Rachael assigned two of the slave boys to be playmates and helpers to her sons. One of the slaves had a little girl who was her namesake, Rachael; she gave her to Marie, who delighted in playing dolls with Little Rachael and had her fix her hair and help her put on her fine little dresses. To Jemmie, she gave a boy named Christian, who helped him with carpentry projects. The one she gave to Alex was named Ajax. Ajax had very little to help Alex with, so Alex wanted to do something for *him*. He began to teach Ajax how to read.

"You see, Ajax?" he was saying one evening. "This is the alphabet. It contains all the letters in the English language that form words." He showed him words and started to read them out loud, talking about how each letter had a sound that, when added to other letters, made words.

"I see, Master Alex. So dis word here, is 'me.' It has da letter 'm' dat is said like 'mm' and da letter 'e' dat is said like 'ee.' So 'mmee' is 'me'!"

"That's correct! You're learning it, Ajax!" He gave his friend a squeeze on his shoulders.

Jemmie came in from the woodshop for a bite to eat. He saw what Alex was doing and told him to stop it. "Slaves don't read," he said, laughing softly and shaking his head.

"Mine will," said Alex. "He's catching on well already. And Maman told me I could do it if I wanted to, isn't that right, Maman?"

"Yes, Alex. Jemmie, leave him alone."

"But Mama, a slave that can read—"

"Will be a very valuable one," Rachael concluded.

Alex smiled.

Shaking his head, Jemmie went back to the woodshop.

"Maman," said Alex. "Isn't it cruel to enslave people? I've seen them out working in the fields and they… well, they whip them, don't they?"

Marie covered her ears and squeaked, shaking her head, sadly.

Rachael sighed. "Yes, Alex. It is cruel. But I'm afraid there seems to be no other way as things stand right now."

At that moment, James returned home. After they greeted him, he said, "So, what were you discussing when I came in?"

"Slavery," said Alex.

James exchanged a look with Rachael and sighed, then sat down in his easy chair. Rachael caught him up on the conversation. "Aye, well…. When people first started to come to these islands from Europe, they did the work themselves, but it proved quite difficult. It still is very hard to make a go of it, even with slaves working for you. The negroes, we have found, are a particularly hardy breed. But, yes, it has proven necessary to… er… motivate them with the use of a whip. I…. Son, honestly, I'm not fond of the practice myself. Unfortunately, it seems the only means by which sufficient productivity can be achieved in order to remain competitive with the other planters."

Alex nodded. "I understand, Papa, but I still don't like it. Sugar is nice and sweet, but I don't feel it's worth the price."

"You're sweet enough, my boy," said Rachael. "You don't need it."

Alex smiled.

"What about me?" asked Marie.

"You're even sweeter," Rachael said, kissing her.

"Yeah, but I still like sugar!" the girl said. Alex couldn't help but laugh, albeit very briefly. When the laughter was over, he was still sad and angry at the injustice of it all.

When the time was right, Rachael and James started to teach their children how to dance. The three youngsters took to it well and often partnered with each other or with the slave children while their mother or father played harpsichord or clapped the timing. The parents wished they could afford to hire a dance master to teach them more.

Rachael and James noticed that although Marie and Jemmie often went outside to play with their friends, Alex always stayed indoors reading. They didn't want to discourage him from continuing his autodidactic habits but felt that he should not eschew the beneficial exercise of his body. Rachael began to take Alex outside with a couple books and sit under a tree with him while they both read. They would take short breaks during which they walked and talked about what they had read.

As these walks grew in length, Alex read passages from his books out loud to his mother. He told her he wanted to memorize certain sections, and so he repeated his favorite passages over and over.   Rachael grew tired of hearing them and stopped walking with Alex. By that time, the walks had become a habit for the boy. He was thereafter seen frequently walking and talking, drilling whole books into his head. Despite being occasionally teased or even bullied for talking to himself, this practice became a lifelong habit of Alexander's. Although it made him look a bit eccentric, it certainly helped him learn more quickly and remember much useful information. Little wonder that he gained the reputation of being a mad genius.

Chapter Five: The Divorce

Rachael's sister Jemima traveled to Nevis and paid her a visit. After the usual pleasantries, she broached a most unpleasant subject: Levine.

"You know, he married his washer-woman fiancée," said Jemima.

"What?" Rachael was shocked.

"I thought you knew that. The divorce—"

"Divorce? What divorce?"

Jemima explained how Levine had filed for divorce. He had asked her for Rachael's address so that a summons could be sent to her and Jemima had given it to him. Rachael paled. That man knew where she lived…?

"When was this?"

"1759."

Rachael calmed down. It had been years. If Levine had wanted to mess with her, he would have done so by now.

Apparently, he was content with his new wife. Good. But… then a thought occurred to her and she brightened. "So, Red and I can marry now!"

Jemima paled. "No. It… uh… the divorce found you at fault and did not free you. Just Levine."

"At fault for what?"

"Abandonment. He claimed you neglected him and his son."

"That's a lie! He kept me away from my son! And as for him, he never loved me. He only wanted to… *humiliate* me." She looked down, blinking back tears.

Jemima patted her hand. "There, there, my dear sister. Oh, I'm so sorry to be the bearer of such evil tidings."

"Can you send me a copy of the court papers? I need to know what they say."

"Certainly. But I'm surprised you didn't get a copy. Unless he—"

"Didn't give the court my address. He probably gave them an old one. He shut me out on purpose. He wanted the court to rule in his favor. He didn't want me to come and defend myself. Even if I had come, he probably would have had me thrown in prison again for… for being with James. And he could have had James imprisoned as well. Oh, God, what might have happened to my children if that had happened?"

"Well, it's all over now, I'm afraid. What's done is done."

Jemima, true to her word, forwarded a copy of the divorce papers to Rachael. James was home when the post arrived. They sat down together. James anticipated what was about to happen: he knew Rachael would be very upset at what she was about to read. He sent the children out to play. They didn't know it, but Alex snuck back and was listening at a window as Marie, Jemmie and the slave children went into the meadow to toss a ball around.

Despite Jemima's warning, Rachael and James were shocked at what they read. The summons had been issued on February 26, 1759. The addresses listed for Rachael were Fort Christianvaern – the prison where she had been incarcerated for seven months -- and the house she and Levine had once lived in, a place she hadn't been to for many years. He had known full well that she wouldn't receive the summons at either place.

In the divorce complaint, Levine had leveled some horrifying charges against her. He claimed that Rachael had made "such mistakes that among married people are indecent and very suspect."

"He's the indecent one! What of the rape?"

"No one knows of it, lass," said James. "And, as he said, husbands have the right to lie with their wives, willing or no'."

"No woman should ever have to lie with a man unless she wishes it, even if he *is* her husband!" Rachael said, vehemently.

They read on.

Levine mentioned her imprisonment for the crime of having twice committed adultery. He wrote that Rachael had been away from him for nine years and had "gone to another place, where she is said to have begotten several illegitimate children, so that this is thought to be more than enough reason to obtain a divorce…. She has shown herself to be shameless, rude and ungodly, as she has completely forgotten her duty and left husband and child alone, and instead given herself up to whoring with everyone, which things the plaintiff says are so well known that her own family and friends must hate her for it."

"Lies!" cried Rachael. "I never sold my body! And 'with everyone'? I've only been with two other men! And my family don't hate me! How can he even say such things?"

James put a comforting arm around her shoulder. "I know. We know. They know. No one hates you but Levine, Rachael. He's a fool and a knave." Rachael leaned on his shoulder, thankful that he could still be so sympathetic with her despite the troubles they had been through.

Levine had written that a divorce was necessary so that Rachael would not be able to "take possession of the estate and therefore not only acquire what she ought not to have but also take this away from his child and give it to her whore-children what such a legitimate child alone is due."

"'Whore-children?!' Good God! Oh, James! How can he say such things? Our children are beautiful. They are not obscene!"

"I know, lassie. Dinna fash over this. No one can look at our children and see anything wrong with 'em."

Following this was a summary of the testimony of three witnesses Levine had had summoned to appear before the court. They appeared in April, including her sister Jemima who testified that she had seen Rachael two years before on St. Eustatius and she had had two children, clearly not Levine's, with another man. They didn't even give James' name, as if he were a non-entity, or perhaps even to imply that no one knew who the real father was. She was just living with some other, unidentified man, not necessarily in a committed, monogamous relationship with him. Rachael was shaking. How dare they speak so of her?

Perhaps the most damning testimony of all had been that of one of the male witnesses who said that Rachael's "common reputation was that she was a public whore."

Rachael dropped the papers and put a hand to her mouth. Shaking, she stood up and ran out the back door of the house. "Rachael…!" said James, running after her. He found her just outside the door, on her knees, vomiting. After she'd finished and recovered enough, he helped her back inside, gave her a towel and a glass of rum.

She said nothing for long minutes, just stared at nothing. She couldn't even shed any tears. She was too stunned. Finally, she came out of the trance. "I can't handle any more of it. You read it."

James did. There was nothing further, however, against her that had not already been stated. He blew out a breath, relieved. "There's nae more here, lass. Nae more to fear."

She shook her head. "It matters not. There's more than enough to damn me in the eyes of anyone who should read this."

"If they believe it."

"Why wouldn't they?"

"They wouldna if they knew Levine and his friends."

"The court believed them!"

James sighed. "Aye. Apparently so."

"How can I live with this, Red? It's public record. Anyone can read it!" She started to sob.

He held her. "Hush, lass. We're on Nevis. No one here will know about this. People here dinna go to St. Croix looking for other people's divorce papers."

Finally, included with the papers was the court's ruling on the matter, dated June 25, 1759. It was just as Jemima had said. Levine was free to marry again; Rachael was not. She and her children could not inherit his estate.

"He'll never amount to anything," said Rachael, laughing bitterly. "So, losing claim to his estate matters not to me, nor to our children. Let Peter get it all. I don't care. 100% of nothing is still nothing."

"He is still your son," said James.

She nodded. "I have never stopped loving him. But no doubt Levine has turned him against me and calls me a 'whore' in front of him. Just think what that kind of thing can do to a boy. To believe such a lie about his own mother!"

James shook his head. "I doubt he believes that about you. He probably hates his father and will leave him soon as he's grown."

"I just can't get over it that that man said I had a reputation as a whore…"

"That's a lie, fed to him, no doubt, by Levine. Nobody says that about you. I would have heard it. If I could find this man, I'd challenge him to an affair of honor."

"Don't say that, Red. I couldn't stand to lose you. I know we've had hard times, but you must know I still love you so very much. I have never stopped loving you and I never will."

He kissed her, not passionately, but

tenderly. "As I love you, Rachael. And I always will."

"Likewise, Red." They held onto each other for a time. Finally, Rachael stood up and stepped outside to call the children back in but saw Alex with his ear up against a window. "Alex…" she called.

He spun around, a guilty look on his face. "Maman!"

"You heard?"

He nodded. She sighed. "We're going to have to have a talk with you."

"I'm sorry, Maman. But I was worried because you seemed upset. I wanted to know why."

"Do you know now?"

"Well… I don't understand everything you said. What's a wh-whore?"

"Come inside."

She told James that Alex had been listening in. "Good God," James swore softly.

"He doesn't understand it all, Red."

"As he shouldna. He's little more than a wee bairn!"

"He's mature for his age. I think we should tell him."

James sat silent for a moment, considering. "You're sure about this?"

"Yes."

He sighed. "Verra well. Go on." He looked away.

"Alex, I was married to a man named John Michael Levine years before I met your father. He was… very cruel to me. He hurt me and did things to me I didn't want him to do. There was a nice man I met named Johan Cronenberg who promised to protect me. I left Levine for him and Levine had me thrown in prison for it."

Alex gasped. "You were in jail?"

"Yes."

Alex couldn't possibly imagine his kind and classy mother in a prison cell.

"In Fort Christianvaern. On St. Croix. I was there for seven long months."

"That must have been terrible!"

"It was."

"But why? If he was cruel to you—"

"It didn't matter. I broke the law. And because I did, Levine called me a 'whore,' which means a woman who does… *things* she isn't supposed to do with men she isn't married to, in exchange for the men giving her money."

"Did Mr. Cronenberg give you money?"

"No."

"So, you're not a whore."

"No. But Levine wanted to convince the court that I was so they would give him a divorce and punish me by not freeing me to marry your father."

"It's a foul, dirty word, 'whore.'" said James. "And you are not to repeat it."

"I won't, Papa. But I thought Maman

was married to you."

James told him about the church wedding. "Do you understand now, son?" James asked.

"I believe so, Papa. Thank you both for telling me this."

"Promise me you won't tell the other children," said Rachael. "Let us keep this secret for now."

Alex nodded. "I promise."

Rachael gave him a hug and a kiss. "Tu es mon petit homme."

Alex beamed. No one had ever called him a "man" before in any language. A "little" man, perhaps, but a man, nonetheless.

Chapter Six: The Loss

Something happened not long after. Something unexpected, something tragic. Worse, even, than being unfairly defamed as a woman of ill repute. Marie suddenly became very ill and had to lie in bed, sweating with a terrible fever. Rachael sent for the doctor, not caring about the expense. He did the usual things: bloodletting and herbal remedies. Nothing worked. The whole family prayed harder than they had ever prayed. Alas, however, nothing helped. Marie wasted away, weaker every day. Rachael sat by her side, sponging water on her forehead, holding her hand, pouring water into her mouth. James sat on the other side. Marie wasn't very conscious of any of this. Finally, she exhaled a weak, rasping breath and her chest froze. Rachael stared with horror. James had been watching as well. Rachael began to sob, louder and louder. She put her head against her daughter's and screamed in agony; the pain was so great. James put his arm over her shoulders and leaned into her. Alexander, in the other room with Jemmie, who was working on a carpentry project, dropped the book he had been trying to read and Jemmie put his handiwork down. The two boys entered the room to see their parents holding their sister, both sobbing. Alex couldn't stop tears from filling his eyes. Jemmie looked at him, his face sad.

Alexander stepped forward and joined his parents in their grief. Jemmie headed toward them, at a loss. He didn't want to cry. He didn't want to give in to his own sorrow. But he couldn't deny to himself that he would miss his sister and was saddened by his parents' grief. He put a hand on Alex's shoulder, which was heaving with his sobs, and the other on his mother's. Tears, unbidden, spilled down his face, too.

In the weeks that followed, Rachael didn't stir from her bed. She seemed to be fading away herself. Alex and the others prayed constantly for her. They couldn't bear the thought of losing her, as well. It was just too much. She hadn't been able to go to her daughter's funeral. James and the boys had handled the terrible task, paying Marie a tender tribute. They had no money for a marker, so Jemmie fashioned a wooden cross and inscribed Marie's name with her years of birth and death on the crosspiece. Alex spoke a few words to eulogize her. He stumbled over his words as he spoke, pausing now and then to sob. At last, he made it through the speech. They all laid wildflowers on top of the little mound of dirt, kissed it, then stepped away.

Rachael had been silent, sleeping most of every day, crying the rest. She wasn't eating much and barely drank any water. Alex couldn't take it anymore. He couldn't just sit idly by and watch her fade away.

"Maman…" he said. "We need you. *I* need you, Maman. Maman? I love you. *Please!* Don't leave me…" His voice broke and he hugged her, kissing her. He backed up to look at her. Her eyes were still closed. "Please, Maman! Don't you dare leave me! Live!" Angry and desperate, he took her by the shoulders and began to shake her. "Wake up, Maman! Do you hear me? For pity's sake! I beg of you! If you won't do it for yourself, then do it for me. *Live! Live, damn you!*"

Her eyes opened and Alex stopped shaking her.

"Alex...?" she said, her voice dreamy. It was the first word she had spoken since the death of Marie.

"Maman!"

"I heard you speaking. Marie is... she's dead." She said it as if suddenly coming to the realization.

"I'm sorry, Maman, but yes."

She nodded. "I have been wandering in dreams. Nightmares. I thought I had died."

"No, Maman. You are fine, yes?"

"I believe so. I am... *hungry.*"

Alex smiled, relieved. It was the best news he could have heard. "I will get you something to eat!"

For a time, Rachael was still weak. But with food and a little more rest, she was well on the road to recovery. She was still sad and more silent than usual. But she would live. In time, she began to resume her education of Jemmie and Alex. Increasingly, it was just Alex, as Jemmie would often be out in the woodshop, further honing his carpentry skills.

Chapter Seven: The Separation

And so, the years passed. Though the pain of their loss faded, it was always with them. Their father would sometimes sink into a depression and was unable to rouse himself to work or to look for work. As a consequence, their financial state continued to decline; more and more treasured possessions needed to be sold off. Gone was the harpsichord. Most of their furniture was gone. Little remained but Rachael's small library of books and her silver tea set, which she also sold off piece by piece until nothing remained but a few spoons. Rachael and James' relationship started to suffer under the strain. Alex noticed this and it frightened him. He felt instinctively that they still loved each other, but they rarely showed it anymore, not like they had in the past.

"We're moving to St. Croix," James announced one day.

"What?" asked Rachael, irritated.

"You heard me, lass."

"Don't take that tone with me, Red."

"I have a job to do. To make us money, like you want. The Ingrams are owed a debt by a man named Alexander Moir, though he denies it. They want me to collect it. So, we'll need to move there. This could take some time. I've already leased a place in Christiansted."

"You did this without me?" Rachael slammed her palm on a nearby table. "I don't even get a say in where we live now, not the location or the house? Do you think I relish returning to St. Croix? Where that son of a bitch lives?"

"Don't start, Rachael. And don't use language like that."

She ignored his reprimand. "No, Red, no! You don't get to make every decision."

"Do I not? I'm the man, the father of your bairns. Get packed, we're going."

"You are becoming more and more like Levine. Whatever happened to the man I loved?" Real pain was in her voice.

"I can't please, you, can I?" His voice

was raw with pain. "No matter what I do, it's never good enough for you, is it?" He headed for the door.

"Where are you going?" she asked.

"To the pub. Where I don't have to listen to you."

"He's gone," said Rachael. "That's it, he's gone." She placed the letter on top of the table. Alexander took it and read it. Then re-read it. It was short and to the point.

My dearest Rachael,

I most deeply and sincerely regret that there have been difficulties between us and believe me, I am most heartfully sorry for all I have done, all I have not done; all I have said, and all I have not said. Know that I have always loved you and always shall. I feel confident you will consider me most cruel for the present course of action I feel compelled to take, but I am certain that it is for the best for you and our bairns.

You must consider yourself to be free of me so that you may find another man who can better provide for you and the boys than this failure of a Scotch immigrant. I know this may take some time, despite your considerable attractive qualities. In the meantime, I am certain that your relations would not leave you without means and, while I deeply regret that I must render you dependent upon their generosity, I see no other viable option at the present time.

If, by some contrivance or miracle, I should finally make my fortune and you remain free, I shall return to you. Forsooth, I must confess that to be my dearest wish. But, for want of any lasting financial success, I must at the present time sever ties, although doing so fills me with pangs the like of which I can scarcely bear. It is my dearest hope that such a situation may be merely temporary.

Adieu, my darling. Yours ever

JH

Several months had passed since they had moved to their new home in Christiansted. James had left on a ship to do a job and, most likely, he would never come back

"Let me see it," said Jemmie. Numb, Alex handed the letter to him.

"He'll come back, won't he, Maman?"

She shook her head. "I don't think so, mon cher. I-I don't think so." Her voice was trembling, and Alex noticed tears welling up in her blue-grey eyes. The eyes that were shaped so much like his own.

"But--"

"It's always the ones you love the most who can hurt you more than anyone." The tears were now streaming down her face. Alex hugged her. Jemmie joined them. For a time, they clung together.

"But he'll come back," Alex said again, through his own tears. "He *must*. He's our father!"

"I don't know. I wish I could say." Rachael leaned back and began wiping the tears from her sons' faces. "Now, you two listen to me. We will make it. We have my family. They'll help us get started. But I'm going to need both of you to be men now. Can you do that?"

They nodded.

"I intend to set up a shop. I was thinking about doing it anyway, even before I received this letter. Now I know I'll have to. I need you to help me."

"I'll do whatever you need, Maman," said Alex.

Jemmie nodded. "So will I."

"My precious boys. You make me so proud." A slight smile curved her lips. Alex had always liked that smile and how it lit up her face. Now it was tinged with poignancy, but, as such, did not make her any less beautiful.

Alex couldn't take it anymore. He broke away and headed out the door. "Alex!" his mother cried out, but he ignored her. He ran down the street and continued running as long as he could. He didn't go far; he had never been an athletic boy. Near the center of town, he slowed to a walk, breathless. Naked slaves, their bodies glistening with oil, were at the market, being inspected and auctioned off. Others, new acquisitions were being whipped, driven into the sugar cane fields; there, most of them would perish from the heat and exhaustion within five years and be replaced by new ones such as these. All to feed the avarice of their white owners. His parents had owned them, and his maternal grandparents. He had eaten food provided for by the spoils from such inhumane enterprise.

The West Indies were crawling with pirates and other criminals. People intent on snatching one's purse, swindling, cheating, fighting, killing. *Is this what it means to be human?* he wondered. *Is there no man I can trust or depend upon? No one whose hands are clean? Are they all fools and knaves?*

There had to be a better place in the world than this. Surely. Surely God wouldn't have created a world and made it such a hell *everywhere.*

If it is ever in my power, he swore, *I will escape these accursed islands.*

The sun was going down. He turned and headed home.

That night, he had trouble sleeping and his mother, figuring he might still be upset, checked in on him.

"Are you okay?" she asked.

He shook his head. "I can't sleep. I miss him."

Rachael sat on the side of the bed and caressed Alex's face. "I know, mon cher. Me too." She thought for a moment. "Would you like to hear a story?"

Storytime had always been Alex's favorite, although he was, perhaps, a little old for it and had long been in the habit of reading for himself. But now, it was just what he needed. "Oui, Maman."

"Once upon a time, there was a boy who, when he was born, looked just like any other boy who had ginger hair and violet-blue eyes."

Alex smiled, cynically. "This isn't a real story, is it?"

"Actually, Alex, this is the realest story of all, mon fils. Yes, he looked much the same as the others, but he was different. You see, this boy had a secret which was so very secret even *he* didn't know it. But his mother knew."

"What was it?"

She leaned closer and whispered, "He was *special.*"

"Special?"

She nodded. "And someday, there would be millions who would know him and love him. For he would make the world a better place."

"Oh, Maman. Can this be true?"

"It will be. One day." She kissed him. "Now sleep, my darling. And the world will seem brighter tomorrow and every tomorrow that follows it." She stood and headed for the door.

"Maman…?" he said as she was about to exit.

She turned. "Oui?"

"It's not much of a story, is it?"

She smiled. "Non. Not much. But then, most of it hasn't been written yet."

Then, he asked her a question, though he already knew the answer. He just wanted to hear her say it. "And who is going to write the rest of it?"

"You are, mon coeur. You are." She closed the door softly behind her.

Alex smiled, closed his eyes and fell deeply asleep.

Chapter Eight: The Shop

Thomas Dipnall rented a store to Rachael along with the living quarters situated above it where she and her boys slept at night and shared their evening meals. Rachael had borrowed an adequate sum of money from her brother-in-law James Lytton and had used it to buy enough inventory to stock the vacant storefront. She paid a deposit and the first month's rent, per conditions she'd negotiated. She also contracted with Nicholas Cruger of the firm of Beekman and Cruger, ordering imported goods and supplies from them as well as from Dipnall. She sold all manner of items, including food, fabric, tools, clothes and other sundry goods not manufactured on the islands. Ships were constantly pulling in and out of the harbor, delivering imported commodities and taking away sugar, molasses and rum.

Rachael's strength in the shop was customer service. She had an easy manner and could relate to people. She noticed Alexander, from time to time, mirroring her as she mingled with the customers, complimenting them, engaging them in conversations designed to discover their desires, then enticing them with what she had to offer. Despite the difficulties in his life, Alexander seemed to be as genuinely interested in interacting with other people as Rachael was herself. Jemmie helped out by making needed repairs to the shop, building and hanging shelves, and similar handiwork.

Rachael was skilled at bookkeeping but had little patience for it and needed time to attend to customers. Early on, she'd asked Alexander if he were interested in helping her keep the books and he'd eagerly agreed. She trained him and, in no time at all, he was doing this exclusively. She'd check his figures every now and then and they were always on the money.

She complimented him. "I'm so glad you're proficient at maths, mon fils," she said. "It helps to have these skills. And your verbal skills are far beyond your years as well."

Alex shrugged. "Thanks to all you've taught me. I like to read and write. It takes me away...."

She hugged him then. "I'm glad you're always accurate with things. It helps..." Her face clouded over. She didn't often speak of her ex-husband, but now felt compelled to do so. "It was not so with Levine. He kept books for his business affairs. I would look at them when he was away and couldn't see me. Abysmal. He cheated. People found out and no one trusted him. That's one reason so many of his business ventures failed. One thing you must promise me, Alexander, is that you will always be honest in your business dealings. Protect your good name and integrity above all. Without being known as an honorable man, you cannot go far. Will you promise me you'll do that?"

"Of course, Maman."

One Saturday, a family entered the shop, a mother, father, son and daughter. They had been there before, and Alex recognized them. The daughter always looked at him. In fact, sometimes she even stared at him. On this particular day, the girl went up to Alex and said, quietly, so as not to be overheard, "I have something for you."

She handed him a note and winked.

Alex was surprised. No one had ever done that to him before. He was still rather young and inexperienced. He read the note. "I like you. Come see me in my backyard tomorrow." It had her address. The shop was closed on Sundays, as were all businesses, for the Sabbath.

The next day, Alex told his mother he wanted to go out for a walk in the woods. This was unusual, but Rachael was happy to hear that Alex wanted to go outside. He needed to exercise more often. He hadn't lied to her. He *was* going to walk through the woods on his way to the girl's house. And then walk back home after… after what, exactly? He had no clue what she wanted to do.

When Alex arrived in the backyard, he saw the girl sitting by the garden, making a crown out of wildflowers. She looked up as he approached. "Hello!" she said. "I'm glad you came. What's your name?"

"Alex," he said.

"I'm Sally. I think you're cute, Alex."

"You do?" He smiled.

"Do you like how I look?"

"Oh, yes, you're very pretty. Like a flower."

She giggled. "Thank you. I like flowers. Do you?"

Alex shrugged.

"Here." She put a flower crown his head and the other on her own. "Now we match."

Alex laughed.

She leaned in to whisper in his ear. "Do you like me?"

He nodded. They sat and talked for a time about their lives. Sally had lived in luxury far beyond anything Alex had ever experienced. He envied her until she started to tell him about how mean her brother Donald had been to her. He had insulted her frequently, telling her she was stupid, and had even punched her a few times. When Alex spoke of his troubles, especially of having lost his sister and father, Sally placed a sympathetic hand on his shoulder.

"I'm so sorry to hear that, Alex. I'm sure you loved them very much." She leaned in to kiss Alex on the cheek. Alex blushed redder than the hibiscus flowers in Sally's garden.

Suddenly, an angry male voice yelled, "Sally, what in the bloody hell are you doing?"

Sally and Alex turned. Sally's brother Donald was stomping toward them.

"I just—"

"What you are doing is wrong! Especially with the likes of him!"

"What's wrong with Alex?"

"Don't you know anything? He's a bastard. His mother is a whore!"

"That's a lie!" said Alex. "My mother is not a whore!"

"Did you just call me a liar?"

"Either that or you are misinformed."

The boy pushed Alex to the ground. He put a knee in Alex's stomach to keep him down. Alex groaned with pain. "You don't talk that way to me, you little bastard. I'm better than you and so is my sister. You stay away from her, do you hear me?" He started to pick up clumps of dirt and threw them in Alex's face. "You don't play with her, you don't talk to her, you don't ever look at her. Do you understand me, bastard boy?"

When Alex didn't answer, the bully grabbed his ear and twisted it. Alex struggled and forced himself not to cry. Donald was much bigger, and Alex couldn't free himself. "I… I *understand* you," he said, hoping that would stop the assault.

"Riffraff like you will never be good enough for her."

That was too much. Donald had stepped over a line and now Alex's pride was engaged. "You're wrong."

"What did you say?" The bully pulled his hair.

Alex moaned. "I said you're wrong."

Donald punched Alex in the face. "Shut up. You shut your hole, you lying bastard!" He turned to Sally and started to yell at her again. The distraction enabled Alex to struggle and free himself.

Donald tried to grab for him, and Alex kneed the bully in the groin. Donald doubled over. Alex stood and began to yell at him. "I *am* worthy of a girl like Sally. And, someday, I'll prove to everyone that *I* am better than *you!*" He blew Sally a kiss and ran away.

Sally laughed and blew him one back.

Despite his bravado, however, tears came to Alex's eyes as he made his way home. The bully's words had wounded him deeply. He *was* a bastard. And nothing would change that. But he was determined. Someday, he would be the greatest bastard who ever lived. Conversely, Donald, and all other bullies, would just be losers like Levine who never amounted to anything.

The door to the store opened and in walked Nicholas Cruger. Rachael was assisting customers, but she looked up and greeted him. "Good morning, Mr. Cruger.

What brings you by?"

"Invoices from your latest orders." He pulled up a leather satchel.

"Take them to my son Alex in the back office, if you wouldn't mind," she told him.

"Not at all, ma'am," said Cruger.

"Thank you for attending to this matter personally, Mr. Cruger."

"Your servant, ma'am."

Rachael liked that he never called her "Mrs. Levine" as many on St. Croix were wont to do. She wanted nothing to do with *that* name, even though, legally, it still belonged to her. The divorce decree had not restored her maiden name to her; for privacy, however, she sometimes used it with various alternative spellings, the most creative of which was "Fatzieth."

Alex recognized Nicholas Cruger as he opened the office door and entered. He had been reading a book, which he now set down. He was a little nervous at seeing the man enter. He stood. "Sir, I am--"

"Master Alex Hamilton, I presume," said Cruger. He bowed. "I am Mr. Nicholas Cruger of--"

"Of Beekman & Cruger, yes, I've heard Maman speak of you." Remembering his manners, Alex bowed back and said, "Pardon my interruption of your most gracious introduction, sir. I am y-your servant, sir." He had made a blunder of courtesy and was afraid of the bad impression he'd made.

"Relax, Alex. Your mother tells me you handle the accounts for the shop. Is that true?"

"Yes, sir."

Cruger lifted the satchel and placed it on an empty space on the table. He opened the case and removed some papers. "I have the most recent invoices here to add to your account. Each has its own pay-by date at the top. Mind you pay promptly, yes?"

"Certainly, sir."

Cruger looked behind Alex to a set of shelves that held a number of leather-bound ledgers. His curiosity was now piqued. "I take it those are your account books."

Alex followed his gaze. "Ah, yes, sir."

"And you have been keeping these all by yourself?"

"My mother did it at first, and then she taught me, and I took over."

"May I peruse them?"

Alex blushed. "Do you suspect us of having errors, sir?"

"Oh, no, not at all. It's just that I've never met someone so young who could keep accounts in order."

"Oh. Well, in that case, let me show you." Not only did Alex hand the books to Cruger, but he opened them and showed Cruger how he had tweaked the system, adding details and notations to further make the transactions clear and easy to follow. Cruger had to admit, the books were not only orderly and accurate, but more informative than even his own firm's accounts. To say he was impressed was something of an understatement.

"Ingenious..." He hadn't meant to say the word. It had just come out.

Alex shrugged humbly. "I'd rather say I am studious and industrious than in sole possession of the Godly gift of brilliance, for I endeavor to apply my attention entirely to any skill I wish to master."

"Clearly." Then an odd thought crossed his mind and he had to follow it to its conclusion. He frowned. "When I came in here, you were reading a book, were you not?"

Alex blushed slightly. "Yes, sir. I had some s-spare time and I love to read."

"Do you often have spare time?"

"Yes, but I usually help Maman in the store when I do. I don't go to school, but I want to learn as much as I can, so I read. And Maman doesn't really need me to help her, although I enjoy doing so. May I be so bold as to ask, what is the purpose of your inquiry, sir?"

Cruger smiled. "My partner David

Beekman and I could use some assistance at our firm. If you are interested and your mother consents, I could engage you in some part-time clerk work. You would learn much about international trade, currency exchange rates, and the like...."

Alex's eyes grew wide. "I am certainly interested, sir. I will have to speak with Maman, as I will require her consent."

As expected, his mother consented, excitedly, saying it would be a great opportunity for him.

Chapter Nine: The Savior

And, just like that, Alex found himself sitting behind a desk at Beekman & Cruger's business office. Cruger gave him a quick tour of the office, which was nothing spectacular, but everything was new to Alex and he gazed about with intense curiosity. One of Cruger's employees gave the boy a small bit of training. Alex picked things up so quickly, it made Cruger's head spin. He gave Alex more and more complex tasks to complete, assigning various employees to continue his training. Some of the firm's older, more experienced employees looked on the boy with a bit of envy for his intelligence, and, perhaps a little resentment as well. But he was so well-mannered and friendly that he soon won them over.

Alex found some aspects of the job a little challenging, but in a good way. He soaked up knowledge as quickly as he could, asking question after question until his trainers grew almost weary of answering them. Many of his questions went way beyond the scope of his work as a clerk.

Alex helped out with the correspondence with customers, suppliers, and the Cruger family's other enterprises which were located in Jamaica, Curaçao, New York City and Bristol, England. On St. Croix, they owned warehouses, ships, and a general store as well as the counting house where Alex was working on King Street ("Kongensgade" in Danish). They sold whatever the locals expressed a need for, if it was obtainable for a reasonable price. A shipment might include various goods such as Albany white pine, pork, codfish, Madeira, and mules. Alex learned how to operate the freight scale they used to weigh the cargo. The scale house was not far from Fort Christiansvaern, where Alex's mother had been imprisoned before.

Occasionally, they even sold that most reprehensible of cargoes (in Hamilton's eyes): *slaves*. He felt dirty whenever he had to so much as copy or record a receipt or invoice associated with such a transaction. He felt somehow soiled by the association, as if he actually *approved,* however tacitly, of the institution of slavery. The sad fact was that there were very few ways of making money on the islands that were not, at least to a small degree, connected with slavery. He had a job to do, like it or not.

One evening, as the sun was going down, Alex was heading home from work. He was preoccupied, thinking of the day's business, and he didn't pay attention to the man who was walking ahead of him. The stranger, however, looked back and saw Alex. The man ducked into a nearby alley and waited for the boy. As Alex began to pass by the alley, the man grabbed him and shoved him, face first, up against the side of a building. He held a knife and pressed it flat against Alex's throat. The cold steel of fear gripped his heart.

"Don't make a fucking sound or I'll slit your throat, boy," the man said. He then pulled Alex's breeches down, exposing his bare buttocks. The man loosened his fly. Alex didn't know what the man was about to do to him, but he was sure it couldn't be good. He felt something hard pressing against him. *Oh, God, what is—*

Then, he heard the click of a gun being cocked and a man with a Scottish burr said, "Let go of my son, *now,* or I'll put a bullet in your head." The voice was firm and menacing, but it wasn't his father's.

Alex sighed with relief as the ruffian released him.

"Go!" the Scottish man said. The would-be rapist fled. Alex pulled up his breeches.

His savior lowered his pistol. "Neddy, are you okay? What are you doing out he—"

Alex turned. "I-I'm not N-Neddy. I'm Alex. Alexander H-Hamilton."

"Oh," said the man. "I see that now. I'm sorry. I thought you were—Well, you look so much like muh son Neddy that I thought you were he. Well, come now. Let me walk you home. It's not safe out here for you. I'm Thomas Stevens, by the way."

"Pleased to make your acquaintance, Mr. Stevens." Alex politely bowed to him.

"Which way is home?"

Alex pointed and Stevens walked by his side. After a time, Stevens asked, "Why were you out here?"

"I'm going home. I work at Beekman

& Cruger."

"The import/export company."

"You know of them?"

"Of course, I do. Who doesna?"

"Oh." They continued to speak on the subject. Before long, they arrived at No. 34 Company's Lane. "Well, I live up here, above my mother's shop."

"I've been here before. Your mother runs the place?"

"Yes. She owns it."

"That's a most unusual occupation for a woman."

Alex smiled. "She is a most unusual woman." He couldn't keep the admiration out of his voice.

They reached the top of the stairs and entered the small apartment. "Maman!"

"Alex!" said his mother. "You're home at last." She had barely glanced up, cooking over the stove. "Really, Cruger shouldn't keep you this late."

Alex stepped forward to kiss his mother. "I've brought a… a friend."

Rachael looked up and saw Thomas Stevens. "Oh. Welcome, sir," she said, curtseying.

"This is Mr. Thomas Stevens. Mr. Stevens, this is my mother, Rachael."

"Pleased to meet you, ma'am." Stevens bowed, removing his hat, respectfully.

"Mr. Stevens. You will excuse me, but I am finishing up cooking supper."

"That is perfectly all right, ma'am."

"Won't you take a seat?"

"Thank you kindly, but I canna stay long."

"I understand. So… how do you know my son Alex?"

His face fell. "I'm afraid, I saved him from a ruffian who was… er… attempting to… assault him."

Rachael dropped the utensil in her

hand into the pan and took Alex by the shoulders. "Dear Lord! Alex, are you all right?"

"I'm fine, Maman. Mr. Stevens stopped him before he could… do anything."

She shook her head. "They send all manner of criminals here to these islands." She turned. "Mr. Stevens, I am in your debt, sir. If there is anything I can do for you, you have but to ask."

"Actually, there is something. I have a son named Edward – we call him Ned or Neddy. He is about Alex's age, and he is… well, quite devoted to his studies. Perhaps a little *too* devoted. I'm hoping he and Alex will like each other. Would it be acceptable to you if I brought him over, say, Sunday afternoon?"

"That would be wonderful, Mr. Stevens. Alex, would you like a new friend?"

"Yes, I would!" said Alex. "Thank you, Mr. Stevens," he said. The man headed for the door. But before he could exit, Alex gave him a hug. "Thank you for saving me!"

"Yes," Rachael concurred. "Thank you for saving my boy!"

Laughing fondly, Stevens returned the hug. "You're welcome. I'll see you Sunday."

"We'll see you then."

After Stevens was gone, Rachael asked Alex. "Now, tell me. What exactly did the man try to do to you?"

Alex told her every detail. Rachael sighed. "Alex. I must tell you. That… *man* was trying to do a truly monstrous thing. He was trying to ravish you. To… *rape* you."

"I don't understand what that means, Maman."

"No, and you shouldn't. You're too young to know about such things. It is not only a means of inflicting pain, but it is also a *violation.* It is truly the worst thing one person can do to another." Her face clouded over with thought, with memory.

Alex noticed. "Maman, have you…"

She looked at him and nodded. "I have. My ex-husband is a terrible person.

He did to me something very similar to what that ruffian tried to do to you."

"Oh, Maman. That sounds awful, but I still don't quite understand."

"Nor should you. But since this has happened, I suppose it is time I told you some things. Oh, I wish your father were here."

She gave him "the sex talk." Needless to say, it made quite an impression on Alex.

"So, I need to do that to a woman when I get married to her to make her enceinte?" he asked, using the French word for "pregnant."

"That's right."

"That's what you and Papa used to do?"

"Yes."

He told her about what he and Sally had done but didn't tell her the girl's name.

"Do you like this girl?" Rachael asked.

He nodded. "She's nice."

"Someday, perhaps soon, you're going to start liking girls in a special way, Alex."

"I just hope they'll like me."

"I'm sure they will." She kissed him on the head. "Now, go tell your brother that supper is ready."

Chapter Ten: The Friend

True to his word, Thomas Stevens arrived on Sunday with his son Ned in tow. Both Rachael and Alex could see the resemblance right away. They were both the same height, build, and had the same hair color. Ned's eyes were blue but didn't have the purplish tint that Alex's eyes had. Their facial features were quite similar as well. Why, they could be *brothers.* In fact, Alex looked more like Ned than he looked like Jemmie!

Ned had brought with him a book on the medical arts and anatomy, which he showed to Alex. Alex also had a medical book which had once been his maternal grandfather's and he gave it to Ned who looked over the book with a gleeful curiosity.

"My grandfather was a physician," Alex said.

"I think I might like to be one as well. What about you?"

"I don't know. Maybe. It certainly is a fascinating field of study. But there are others that interest me as well: government, law, history, economics, the military…"

Ned laughed. "You don't want to just pick one?"

Alex shrugged. "Why? When they are all so very important. The more knowledgeable you are, the more useful. I want to be the most useful man ever."

"That sounds like a lot of hard work."

"I'm not afraid to work hard. Anything worth accomplishing in life takes hard work and dedication."

"I study hard, so I'll be a hard-worker as well."

"You could even be the best doctor ever."

"And you'll be the best… everything else!"

"Unless I decide to become a doctor too. At which point, *I'll* be the best physician in the world!"

The two boys began to laugh. Watching them together, Rachael shook her head as another realization hit her: Not only did the two boys look like each other, but they *acted* a lot alike.

From that point on, they were the best of friends. They soon discovered that they both spoke French. Ned had learned it at a school his father had sent him to, as well as Latin and Greek. Alex didn't know many words in those two languages. Ned started to teach him the Greek alphabet and a few Latin quotes.

From that point on, whenever Alex had a spare moment, he would go over to the Stevens house or Ned would come and visit the Hamilton's loft. Alex would usually bring Ajax with him, whose reading ability was improving in leaps and bounds. Ajax had also found an insatiable love for reading among the bounty of the Stevens' library. Almost immediately, the three boys were practically inseparable during their free time. Ned would bring new books to Alex that he had never seen before. They ran the gamut of the subjects Alex had expressed interest in. He also made the acquaintance of Ned's four siblings, but he never bonded with any of them quite as much as he had with Ned.

One day, the two boys had been talking about books and other things. It was a pleasant, beautiful day outside, without a cloud in the sky. "Ned," Alex said, staring pensively out the window, "let's take a walk." It was uncommon for them to do so, but not unheard of. They had taken a few short strolls together, soaking up the beautiful, verdant, tropical paradise of the island. Ned nodded and followed his friend. As they walked, they spoke about history as well as their plans for the future.

Alex led him to a stream in the woods. He pulled out a knife. Ned was slightly shocked. "What is that for?"

"There is a ceremony for something called 'blood brothers,'" Alex said. "I wish for us to be bonded in that way, Neddy. You are like a brother to me, you know. You feel that way about me, yes?"

"Oui. How is it done?"

"We each make a small incision on our hands. Then we join them together and let our blood mingle. We will then be of the same blood. And we make oaths to each other."

Ned smiled. "Let's do it."

Ned took the knife and made a shallow cut in his palm. He passed the knife to Alex, who did the same to his. They clasped hands.

"Repeat after me," said Alex. "I solemnly swear eternal friendship and brotherhood to you."

Ned repeated his words.

"Nothing will end my friendship for you."

"Our blood has mingled. We are family. We are brothers."

"It is done."

They unclasped their hands and looked for a moment at each other. They hugged. Ned sat on the grass and Alex sat next to him.

"You like girls?" Ned asked.

Alex shrugged. "I do, but they're strange sometimes." He told Ned about

Sally.

"Wow. A girl kissed you?"

Alex laughed. "Just on the cheek. I'd like to know what it's like to kiss one on the lips."

"Me too."

"Some boys would go kiss a slave girl to find out what it's like. And then some. I don't think that's right. A girl should *want* to be kissed by you – and the other things…"

Ned nodded. "It's horrible, what they put them through. I wish there was another way. Some people think that's why God inflicts terrible, incurable fevers upon us. As punishment."

"I don't think that's the case. Do you?"

"No. I think it's scientific. But I don't think God likes slavery."

Alex talked about his family's slaves and how well they treated them. How they cared about them too much to sell them to someone who might abuse them.

"I suppose that's better," said Ned, "but still, they're not free. They don't have any choice over their destiny."

"Sometimes, I feel the same way about myself. If only I could get out of these islands, go to the American continent or Europe, and attend college. Or maybe I could join the military and prove my worth there so I could move up in the ranks."

Edward patted Alex on the back. "You'll find a way, Alex. If anyone can, you can."

Alex smiled. "Thanks. I wish I had your optimism."

"You will, someday. You'll see." He stood. "Let's head back, brother."

"Oui… mon frère."

Chapter Eleven: The Past

It was a Saturday, and Alex was helping his mother with the shop. Rachael was in the storehouse behind the building, getting ready to re-stock some shelves. A man walked in. Something about the man made the hairs on the back of Alex's neck stand up. The stranger's clothing had once been fine, but the colors had faded, and the fabric had been torn and repaired - poorly at that - many times. The look would have been comical, had it not been for the sour expression on his face. He reeked of alcohol, tobacco ash, and… laudanum? How long had it been since the man had bathed? His attempt to cover his foul odors with a cheap cologne only made matters worse.

The man looked at Alex, his expression haughty. Was it Alex's imagination, or did the man know he was a bastard? That was the look in his eyes. Like he was judging Alex to be less than human and not worthy of any respect. He had seen that look before, in the eyes of Sally's brother, and a few others who had known of Alex's illegitimacy. Who in the blazes did this man think he was?

That question was answered all too quickly. Rachael emerged from the back. She took one look at the man and dropped the goods she was carrying. Fortunately, they weren't breakable. Alex rushed to pick them up. Rachael stood speechless, stunned, staring at the man.

"Well, well, well," the man said. "So… what they said was true. I just had to come and see it for myself. Instead of opening her legs, the whore has opened a shop." He laughed, cruelly.

Alex whirled. He raised a fist and tried to approach the man, but Rachael held him back. "How dare you talk that way to my mother!"

"I knew it the moment I saw you," said the man. "You're one of her whore-children."

"Get out of my shop, Levine," Rachael said through clenched teeth. Alex was stunned. This was his mother's ex-husband! The horrible monster he had heard so many terrible things about. Like a troll or a goblin from a horror story, he was here to try to torment his mother. *Not if I can help it,* Alex thought.

Levine smiled and started pushing items off the shelves. Rachael grabbed a cane and brandished it. "Don't you dare touch anything of mine! Leave now, or I will call the constable and have *you* thrown in prison!"

Levine scoffed. "I don't give a damn what you do. I have a new family now. And no whore-children." He looked at Alex again, with contempt. "Go on and live your life. But you'll never change what you are deep down inside, and you know it. *Both* of you."

"That goes *double* for you!" said Rachael. "Lying, cheating rapist."

Levine tried to grab the cane out of Rachael's hands, but she held on to it with an iron grip. Alex helped her. Levine released it. "You're not worth the effort, anyway. Neither of you. Scum." He spat and left.

Rachael breathed a sigh of relief, then fell to the floor, sobbing. Alex took her in his arms and comforted her. "It's okay, Maman. He's gone now."

"I hope someday you marry a good woman, Alex. Promise me you will."

"I will, Maman. I promise."

Chapter Twelve: The Orphan

One day in February of 1768, the door to the office burst open and Alex received an unexpected visitor: Ajax. Mr. Cruger, concerned, followed the young slave to Alex's desk.

"Master Alex," said Ajax, his voice filled with consternation. "It's your mama. She's not well. You must come quickly, run the shop!"

"It's fine, Alex," said Cruger. "You may leave. Your work here can wait until later."

"Thank you, Mr. Cruger." He was already following Ajax out the door.

"What's wrong with her?" he asked.

"She got da fever."

The thought filled Alex with dread. The islands were frequently plagued with tropical illnesses, many of which were – sadly – *fatal*. He tried to calm his nerves, but nothing worked. His mother couldn't be sick, she *couldn't* die! He'd be orphaned.

And then what? No, it was too horrible a possibility to even contemplate. *It will be okay,* he thought, trying in vain to reassure himself. *Oh God, Maman, please!* Thoughts of dread and despair raced through his head. He couldn't stop them.

Despite his best efforts, his lips trembled, his eyes filled with tears. Ajax looked at him and put a reassuring hand on his shoulder. "Don't you worry yourself, Master Alex. I'm sure she'll be fine."

Alex nodded perfunctorily, but he didn't feel it. He just couldn't shake the fear whirling inside of him. When they arrived at the shop, Alex saw his mother and his hopes fell. She had closed the shop. She sat in a chair with her head in her hands. When the door closed behind Alex and Ajax, Rachael looked up. Her face brightened, slightly.

"Oh, mon fils," she said, quietly, with none of her accustomed strength, but no less than the usual tenderness. "Can you take over here and reopen the shop? I must go upstairs and get some rest. I'll be fine, though, soon. You'll see."

"Certainement, Maman." Alex did his

best to keep his tone casual and hopeful.

She stood and went to him. She took his face in her hands and kissed him lightly. "That's my smart young man." She turned to Ajax. "You can help him, can't you?"

"Of course, Missus!" said Ajax. "But, first, let's get you upstairs."

Alex and Ajax helped her climb the stairs and settle into bed. They sent for a nurse named Ann McDonnell to help Rachael get better.

But she didn't get better. She only got worse. Much worse. And, as Alex struggled to keep the shop going, he started to feel unwell himself. He frowned and touched his forehead. It was burning up. *No, no, no, no, no, NO,* he thought, panicking. *I can't get this too!*

"You okay, Master Alex?" asked Ajax, concerned.

"I'm fine. Let's get that inventory unloaded." He reached for another crate. As he carried it across the room, he felt his knees suddenly weaken and buckle. He dropped the crate and fell to the floor.

"You're not fine, Master Alex," said Ajax. "You're ill. You need to go upstairs and rest with your mama."

"No, no," Alex protested. "I can work. I can—" He struggled to stand but fell back. Ajax put his hands under Alex's arms and lifted him upright.

"I'm taking you upstairs."

Alex protested, but he was too weak to resist. Ajax yelled for help and the nurse came down. Once they'd managed to bring him upstairs, Alex collapsed into bed beside his mother. She looked over at him, listless and barely conscious.

"Mon fils…?" she said, weakly.

"He got da fever, too, it looks like," said Ajax.

What followed was pure hell for Alex. Nightmare images flooded his mind. In his delirium, he dreamed of his mother, her face bone white, her eyes open, not seeing the maggots and worms consuming her head until nothing remained but a gaping skull.

"Maman!" he cried out, awakening. He looked over. She was still there, breathing slowly, sleeping, her face and body drenched. "Oh, Maman," he said, snuggling next to her and trying to hug her, but he didn't have the strength. He fell back into a troubled sleep.

Dr. Heering came. He bled Rachael and gave them fever medicine to drink. He asked Ann to fetch a chamber pot and gave both Alex and Rachael an emetic. Before long, they were both vomiting into the pot. Rachael begged for water, which Ann promptly gave her. But she seemed only to weaken further. Dr. Heering returned the next day. "Ann," he said to the nurse.

"Yes, Doctor?"

"Ask Dipnall if he can have a chicken slaughtered. Make some broth from it."

"Right away," she said, leaving.

The doctor gave Rachael an infusion of valerian root. He covered her head with alcohol. He bled Alex and gave him an enema. When the ordeal was over, the boy fell asleep.

When he awoke, it was late. Darkness was showing through the open window. Rachael was moaning weakly. "Ann… water… *please….*" she begged. The nurse gave her a cup to drink. There was a bowl of broth on the table, mostly full. Ann poured another bowl and gave it to Alex. He took a few swallows but that was all he could manage.

"Would you like me to fetch the doctor?" she asked Rachael.

Rachael nodded. "Yes, please." The woman left.

Rachael looked at Alex, deep into his eyes. She kissed him. "Oh, mon fils," she said, her voice raspy despite the water. "Such a smart, beautiful boy. I need you to remember something."

Alex closed his eyes. She took his face in her hands. "Look at me." Her eyes were intense, even a little manic. He stared into those depthless orbs.

"Your father was the true husband of my heart. Despite it all, I still love him. I hope that he can take care of you, but if not, I want you to take care of him, if you can,

Alex."

"Maman..." She was saying goodbye to him! He *knew* it! Tears filled his eyes.

"You may be called many unpleasant things in this life." Her breathing was ragged, but she persevered. "Bastard, whore-child, obscene." She laughed weakly and bitterly. "None of it is true. You will be judged unfairly, told you are nothing, not good enough. None of that is true. *Listen to me*…" she whispered, urgently. "We didn't just name you after your grandfather, the laird. We named you after Alexander the Great. You must get better and pursue your dreams. And Alex…?"

"Yes?"

"Promise me you will never forget this: you are not inadequate for the world. The world is inadequate for you."

"I will remember, Maman. I promise."

She sighed and lay back, as if the effort used to speak had cost her the last of her strength. "I love you, my dearest, precious Alexander. I love you so very much. Beyond words, beyond life itself. And I will love you forever."

"I… I love you too, Maman."

"Je t'aime, mon coeur… Alexander…" her voice was barely audible now.

He held her, tears streaming unchecked down his face. "Maman, no… *don't leave me! Please!* I'll do anything! *Please!*" His words fell on deaf ears.

Rachael's head fell back and her breathing shallowed and slowed. He watched the rising and falling of her chest, praying for it to continue. But the breaths came farther apart, until, finally, they ceased. The last breath was exhaled in a long, drawn-out rattle. Her eyes opened, staring at nothing. Just like in that nightmare….

Alex shook her gently, though he knew it would be in vain. "Maman?" he asked, quietly. He shook her as hard as he could. *"Maman!"* But he knew she was gone.

"Help!" he cried out as loud as he could muster.

Ann had just returned with Dr.

Heering. He checked Rachael's pulse and respiration. He looked at Alex. "I'm sorry, son. She's gone." He pulled out his pocket watch and recorded the time of death.

A deep well of grief and despair rose up in Alex's heart and swallowed him whole. He knew no more.

He was rudely awoken by the nurse. "Master Alex, I am truly sorry, but I must prepare the body."

"What...? I don't understand."

She looked down on him, her face an expression of sympathy. "Your mother is—"

"Dead! I know!"

Ann took the pillows off the bed and arranged them on the floor. "Please lie down here while I do this."

He let her help him do so. He closed his eyes and could hear her removing his mother's clothing and the sound of splashing water as she washed the body. *The body. The corpse. Oh, God, please help me!*

That was when *they* came. The vultures. Men. Strangers. They looked at everything, wrote it down. His mother's body was just lying there, naked, and these men came right in. Was there no decency in the world? Had he the strength, he would have fought them off, made them leave. At least until she was concealed in the shroud.

"What are you doing?" Alex asked. "Who are you?"

"We're from probate. We're sealing all of this for auction."

"But it's *ours*. I mean, it belongs to my brother and me now.*"*

"That will be up to the court to decide."

Thomas Dipnall, the landlord, entered with his clerk. Alex recognized the man. "Don't worry, son, I'll make sure you and Jemmie are taken care of."

"Do you know where he has been?"

"With Thomas McNobeny, a carpenter, I believe, as his apprentice. He's been there ever since he heard about the illness, for his own protection. How are you feeling? Physically?"

"Weak. Fevered."

"Hang in there, son."

When they packed up his precious books, Alex mustered his strength and protested.

"No! Those are mine!"

"Just calm down, son."

"Don't take my books!" Alex fought back tears. He tried to stand, but he fell back, exhausted.

"Everything must be sealed." They locked up most of the possessions in the attic and left.

Finished with the bathing, the nurse enclosed Rachael's corpse inside of the shroud and sewed it shut. The undertaker and an assistant came for Rachael and took her away, leaving Alex with nothing.

Ann helped him back into bed. She gave him a pat on the shoulder as if that would help to allay his grief, then exited the room to give him privacy. Clutching a pillow, he sobbed out his grief until he fell into a dreamless slumber.

The next day, Dipnall sent eggs, bread, and cakes for the boys. Alex could barely eat. He choked down a small amount of egg before putting his fork down. After finishing a full breakfast, Jemmie helped Alex into a waiting carriage. They rode behind the hearse. Alex was feeling slightly better, physically, despite it all. His fever had broken, finally. He was still a little weak and queasy, however. Concerned relatives and friends were pitching in, helping the boys through this troubled time. They were given veils to hide their tears and Jemmie received a new pair of dress shoes. Alex certainly needed the veil. He couldn't see Jemmie's face, but he was sure his brother was weeping as well. They had both loved their mother very much.

They made the journey of two miles to the Grange plantation. Even though their uncle James Lytton had sold the property years before, he had retained use of the family's burial grounds. They stopped before a plot under some mahogany trees, in view of the beautiful turquoise sea. A small group of people awaited the boys: Reverend Cecil Wray Goodchild, Uncle James, his daughter Ann's little girl - whom he had temporary custody of - and his son Peter. Standing with his family, Ned Stevens looked at his friend with sympathy. Alex wished his father could have been there. He missed him and he knew that the man must surely still love his mother as she had loved him. But there had not been enough time to get word to him.

The reverend began to speak. "Dearly beloved brothers and sisters, May the eternal God bless and keep us, guard our bodies, save our souls and bring us safe to the heavenly country, our eternal home, where the Father, the Son, and the Holy Ghost reign, one God for ever and ever."

Everyone said, "Amen."

"In this moment of sorrow, the Lord is in our midst and consoles us with his word. No eye has seen, nor ear heard, nor the human heart conceived, what God has prepared for those who love him. Blessed are the sorrowful; they shall be comforted.

Into your hands, O Lord, we humbly entrust our sister Rachael. In this life you embraced her with your tender love and opened to her the gate of heaven. The old order has passed away, as you welcome her into paradise, where there will be no sorrow, no weeping nor pain, but the fullness of peace and joy with your Son and the Holy Spirit for ever and ever."

"Amen."

The reverend read some appropriate passages from the Bible and delivered a short eulogy. Alex barely heard any of it. He couldn't look at anyone. He could only stare at his mother's coffin. Part of him wished he could pry it open and climb inside with her and just lie there until his body faded into nothingness and his soul flew free of all earthly concerns. But he remembered her last words. She wanted him to live. Very well. He would have to live, but for now, his heart was completely consumed with pain, with the loss of the one he had loved above all. He had lost too much in the short time he had been alive thus far. It was almost overwhelming. Once upon a time, he had had a family, a happy one even though they were far from wealthy. Then they had lost his sister, his father, and now this. He and

Jemmie were all that was left. He was even losing Ajax. What was to become of his dark little friend? Would they forbid him to ever read again and force him into hard labor? Maybe even the dreaded cane fields…!

For that matter, what's to become of me? Where am I to go now?

His weakened condition, and the grief weighing him down, finally overcame him and he fainted.

Chapter Thirteen: The Guardians

When he awoke, he was in a strange place, in bed. Jemmie was by his side. "Hey, Alex. Are you feeling all right?" Jemmie's voice was quiet and sympathetic.

Alex looked at his brother. "Where am I?"

"Cousin Peter's. He agreed to take us in. That's a relief, right?"

Alex nodded.

"Just relax, brother. You need to get your strength back. Would you like some soup? I think Ledja is making some."

"Okay. I'll try to eat."

Ledja was Cousin Peter's black mistress. They had a son, Don Alvarez de Valesco, whom everyone called "Al." He came in with a steaming bowl of soup and put it down on Alex's nightstand. "You eat, yes?"

"Thanks, Al," Alex said.

Alvarez smiled, "My pleasure, Alex."

He ate. Not much, but it was a start. He slowly started to recover his strength.

His mother's belongings were auctioned off. Gone now were her coveted silver spoons, her slaves, even her clothes. But the books…

… were somehow sitting on a shelf in the room!

"How…?" Alex asked Jemmie.

"Peter brought them in. He and Uncle James bought them at the auction."

For the first time since his illness, Alex smiled. He picked up a book. It was his favorite volume of poems by Alexander Pope. He caressed the book like it was a pet and closed his eyes, savoring its familiar scent. "I must thank him. Where is he?"

Jemmie shrugged. "He took a business trip off the island, as he does from time to time."

"I'll thank him the next time I see him. These books mean so much to me."

Jemmie smiled slightly and shook his head. "You and your books, Alex."

Alex shrugged. "They've opened the world to me."

"I'm satisfied with this world here in the islands."

"You wouldn't go away if you could?"

"Probably not. Who knows? But you seem to want to."

"I do. I feel my destiny lies elsewhere."

"Maybe. But in the meantime, you're here. And Cruger has been around asking when you'll be able to return to work."

"Maybe in a couple of days. I'm getting stronger. I would like to return to work. I need to, I know."

He had to feel alive again. Working would help. Even if it was just as a lowly clerk.

"What about the slaves?"

"Archibald Hamm bought them all. At least he doesn't have to pay us their salaries anymore. They're now living at his house. They were working for him, anyway, so little has changed. Except that now the children can live with their mothers. Which is better for them because they'll get to see each other every day, not just on Sundays."

"Yes. I just hope they let Ajax keep on reading. He enjoys it so much."

Jemmie shrugged. "Maybe. Oh, by the way, they posted us a copy of the court's findings." He removed a piece of paper from his pocket and handed it to Alex, who read it over. It was in Danish, but by now, Alex knew enough of the language, having acquired such knowledge from living on a Danish-owned island and working for Cruger over the years. It mentioned them as well as their half-brother Peter Levine as being the sole heirs.

"It says we're 15 and 13 years old. We're not that old. Where did they get this information?"

Jemmie shrugged. "Not a clue."

Alex thought for a moment. "Does Peter have Maman's legal papers?"

"I think so."

"Bring them to me."

James left the room and rummaged around elsewhere. He returned with a stack of papers. Most of them related to her business, but near the bottom of the pile Alex found what he was looking for: the divorce papers. He showed Jemmie the testimony from Jemima Gurley.

"Aunt Jemima said Maman had had two children aged 5 and 3 when she visited two years before this hearing."

"But that was Marie and I, not you."

"Yes. So the court must have taken these ages as 7 and 5 during the hearing, which was almost 9 years ago and they added 8 years, making us 15 and 13. They assumed the two children referred to in the hearing were you and I."

"I guess it doesn't really matter. Do you think we'll get any of the money?"

"I hope so. By rights, they should

split it three ways."

Subsequently, Alex made some inquiries and found that the disposition of the estate's assets – that is to say, the money raised at the auction – could be contested until August and the money was therefore being held in escrow by the court. Time went by. When August came around, the boys found out through Cousin Peter that their mother's ex-husband John Levine had filed a motion with the court. Peter attended the hearing on their behalf and had quite an earful to tell them afterward.

"That man is a right nasty piece of work!" Peter said.

"That he is," Alex agreed, recalling the time he had briefly encountered the man one day at his mother's shop.

"He had the audacity to call you 'whore-children!'"

Jemmie was startled by the expression. "That's a lie!"

Having heard it before, Alex merely sighed, shaking his head.

"He said you had no right to inherit

so much as a farthing. That it should all go to his son Peter as the only legitimate heir.”

“Who is now living in South Carolina,” said Alex.

“So, what did the court decide?” Jemmie asked.

Peter looked down, shaking his head. “I’m sorry, lads, but they ruled in Levine’s favor. You get nothing.”

Alex clenched his jaw. “*What?* That’s not fair!”

“Alex, calm down—” Jemmie began.

“No! Peter hardly even *knew* her. We were living with her. We were dependent on her. We *loved* her!”

Jemmie put his hand on Alex’s shoulder, but Alex shrugged him off. “Don’t try to calm me down! We get nothing because we’re *illegitimate?* That’s not our fault!”

“Alex, Jemmie. For what it’s worth, you can stay here as long as you need to.”

“We appreciate it, Cousin Peter. But

it's *wrong*. It's bad enough that we lost our mother, but we also get nothing! Where would we be without you to give us a roof over our heads? "

"I know, but… it's the law," Peter said. "Right or wrong, it is what it is." He looked sad as he said this, as if there were things he'd left unsaid.

"Well, the law should be different. It should be fair. If I had any say in it…."

"Maybe you should study the law, then, brother," said James.

"Maybe I should."

Life was somewhat informal at Cousin Peter's home. He was kind to Alex and Jemmie when he was home but tended to lapse into quiet moroseness. He had lost his wife, whom he had loved very much. He had once enjoyed all the comforts and luxuries that life on the islands had to offer; but, now, his fortunes had taken a considerable downturn and he had had to sell off many possessions that he had prized at one time. The home was taken care of by Ledja. Business concerns often took Peter away from St. Croix, so Alex and Jemmie were better acquainted with Ledja and her son.

Alex didn't see much of Jemmie, either, in those days. His brother was more often than not working as an apprentice for "Old Man McNobeny." He was learning more and more every day. Alex continued to visit the Stevenses whenever he wasn't working. He even spent the night there on occasion. He always looked forward to staying over in Ned's room; they would joke with each other every night before falling asleep.

Now that the shop was gone, Alex was working for Cruger full time. He started to take on more and more of a leadership role. The other employees, most of whom were older than he, had bristled a bit at first to this, but once they got used to Alex's knowledge and fairness in leadership, they accepted and respected his commands.

One day in July of 1769, Alex awoke to the explosive sound of a pistol firing. He jumped out of bed and ran in the direction of the master bedroom, from which the sound of hysterical screaming was coming. Ledja was in the bed, holding on to Peter, and there was blood, so much blood, on the bed and on Peter's clothing.

"Oh, he dead, he dead!" Ledja cried out, sobbing.

Alex didn't have to examine the body to be sure. He could see that there was far too much damage to the brain for his cousin to survive.

Peter had left everything to his mistress and son in his will. Once again, the Hamilton boys were left with nothing.

They had never seen Uncle James looking so haggard and… well… *old.* His face was impassive as he stood over his son's grave and wept silently through the memorial service. "I'll take you home and take care of you," he told the boys. *But who will be taking care of whom?* Alex wondered.

Uncle James had domestic slaves and nurses attending him night and day. He kept to his bed. This was understandable to Alex. He hoped his uncle would recover. He was a kindly old man. Alex had fond memories of him. In the end, that was all he was left with. Uncle James never did recover. In about a month, he, too, was buried at The Grange with his son and Alex's mother.

What now? Alex thought. *Must Death persistently stalk my heels until no one is left?*

Alex and Jemmie spent a few more days being tended to by Uncle James' slaves. But they knew that time was running out and that the slaves were going to be auctioned off along with their uncle's home and all his possessions. His will, too, had left them nothing. This was a condition Alex was sadly getting all too familiar with. He and Jemmie had received nothing from their mother, their cousin, and now, their uncle. It was as if being illegitimate was somehow an unpardonable sin and they could never wash its taint off of themselves. As if they had been the ones to… But, no, he didn't blame his mother and father.

Over the years, he had continued to write his father, of course. He occasionally heard back. James had written that he would have loved nothing more than to provide a home for his boys but, alas, such was far from possible. He was struggling enough to keep a roof over his own head and food on his table. Despite the fact that he still loved them and missed them terribly, it would be unfair of him to take them in when, "there are others upon whom Providence has shined a brighter light than your poor father, those fortunate others who have the means necessary to provide for two growing boys."

Alex was re-reading the latest letter from his father when Jemmie came in. "Old Man McNobeny agreed to give me lodgings during the rest of my apprenticeship. He said you can share the bed with me if you do some work for him too."

Alex nodded. "I suppose that's something. Or maybe Cruger will agree to let me sleep at the office for some extra work."

"That would probably be for the best."

"I suppose." Alex was glum. Neither

option appealed to him.

Alex was at the Stevens home, reading a book, as usual, trying to concentrate despite the uncertain future he faced. Neddy was next to him on the sofa. Mr. and Mrs. Stevens entered the room.

"Alex," Mr. Stevens said.

The boys looked up.

"Mrs. Stevens and I have been talking and we are in agreement. We would like to ask you if you and your brother would like to come here and live with us."

"Do you mean it?" Alex asked, jumping up excitedly. "Truly?"

"Truly," said Mrs. Stevens, laughing delightedly.

Alex ran to the Stevenses and embraced them. Neddy joined in. "Of course!" said Alex. "Thank you, thank you, thank you so much. God bless you both!"

"We'll truly be like brothers, living together and all," said Ned.

"At least until you go off to college," Alex said.

Unfortunately, for Alex, Ned's impending departure for his schooling on the American mainland was not very far in the future; in fact, it was mere months away. Alex and Ned relished the time they had left together. Alex had never been so close to his friend. Before long, however, they were to be torn apart.

When the time for Ned's departure came, they had a tearful farewell at the docks. Ned hugged and kissed his mother, father, and siblings, as well as Alex. "I'll try to come back for the holidays," Ned promised.

"God save you on this voyage," his father said, "and all voyages to come."

"Thank you, Papa."

"Make us all proud."

"I will."

Alex was choked up. He couldn't speak. He was losing his best friend. Certainly, they would write each other, but it wouldn't be the same. He held back tears.

He wished he could go with Ned. He desperately wanted to go to college, too. Dammit, why was life so unfair to him? Why had God given him such a clever and inquisitive mind, only to stifle it with the lack of any significant opportunity to fill it?

Ned boarded his ship and the crew set sail for New York. Standing out on desk, he waved and stared at his loved ones. They all waved back, tears streaming down their faces.

In addition to missing Ned, Alex had to admit to himself that he had grown to hate the job he had and almost wanted to quit. Cruger occasionally gave him added responsibilities, which helped, but the longer he worked as a clerk, the more he felt that the job wasn't a good fit for him. Frustrated, he unburdened himself to Ned in a letter one evening in November. "Ned, my Ambition is prevalent that I contemn the grov'ling and condition of a Clerk or the like, to which my Fortune &c. condemns me and would willingly risk my life tho' not my Character to exalt my Station. Im confident, Ned that my Youth excludes me from any hopes of immediate Preferment nor do I desire it, but I mean to prepare the way for futurity."

He could see no means of advancing himself but through the military. Without money, college was not a possibility, and his career options were severely limited. If only he could somehow get a commission and then be promoted through the ranks. Ultimately, someday, he hoped to be a general. Or, perhaps, if recruited to a naval force, an admiral. He continued the letter.

"Im no Philosopher you see and may be jusly said to Build Castles in the Air. My Folly makes me ashamd and beg youll Conceal it, yet Neddy we have seen such Schemes successfull when the Projector is Constant. I shall Conclude saying I wish there was a War." He was a little young for it, as of yet, but wars tended to last for at least a few years. Pirates roamed the seas, and the occasional slave uprising was a perpetual threat, but other than that, there was relative peace in the islands at that time.

Ned wrote Alex, having much to tell him about New York City and his school, Kings College. He wrote about his teachers and fellow students. He described the city and how there were people from all over, speaking many different languages living there. He wrote about the cold winters and that odd meteorological phenomenon: snow. Alex read these letters with relish and, admittedly, with some degree of envy. Above all, he missed his friend and wished he could be there with him.

Alex had once had a family. Now, they were all gone. The Stevenses were kind to him, and their children provided some companionship. But they weren't *his* family. Alex was lonely.

One Sunday morning, Alex was relaxing, reading a book in the living room when a young man arrived at the Stevens' home. A servant had fetched Mr. Stevens, who escorted the man into the living room. Alex looked up from his book. When Alex saw the man, there was something familiar in his facial features, but he swore he had never seen the man before. He was attractive and quite smartly dressed.

"I'll leave the room to you two gentlemen," Alex said, standing up.

"Actually, this gentleman is here to see *you,* Alex," Mr. Stevens said. "May I introduce Mr. Peter Levine. He says he's your brother."

Alex gasped. So, that was why the man had looked slightly familiar. He could see it now: some of the man's facial features reminded Alex of the mother they had had in common.

"I am pleased to meet you, brother," Peter said, with a polite bow. His accent was mostly that of a St. Croix native, but there was a little something different about it as well. Perhaps it was the influence of living in Carolina.

"The pleasure is mine," Alex replied, bowing back.

"May we speak?"

"Of course. Won't you have a seat?"

Peter sat on the sofa and Alex sat next to him.

Mr. Stevens excused himself, giving them their privacy.

"I have heard that you live in South

Carolina."

Peter nodded. "In Beaufort. I'm a merchant there. My father informed me that it is necessary for me to claim my inheritance in person. No doubt he secured it for me so I would give some of it to him." Peter shrugged and smiled wryly. "I'll only keep enough to cover my travel expenses. I heard from some locals that you were living here. I have always been curious about you. And our other brother, er… Robert?"

"James."

"My apologies. James. He is not here?'

Alex told him about the apprenticeship.

"Ah. I see."

There was a brief awkward silence. Alex could tell that Peter was trying to work up the courage to say something. "I… I wanted to ask you about our mother."

Oh. That. Alex paused, not sure what to say, and Peter went on.

"I haven't seen her for years. I was

very small when..."

"She left you."

"I do not blame her. The circumstances were… insurmountable." Peter sighed. "I know it is wrong to speak ill of one's father, but Papa was… abusive to Mama. When she left, it broke my heart." His voice broke on the last word. "As, I am sure, it did hers. Back then, I didn't understand why she did it, but now I think I know: she didn't want me to grow up to be like Papa. And I… I didn't turn out like him. I'm married to a wonderful woman. We are very happy, and we have a beautiful daughter, Joanna."

"I'm glad to hear it."

"What was it like for you? Growing up with her?"

"She was very loving and generous. She was my teacher, for the most part. We had a happy home; I had a mother and father, a sister and brother."

"A sister? There was no daughter listed in the probate record."

Alex told Peter about Marie.

"I am sorry to hear of her death." He paused, respectfully. "Was your mother happy with your father?"

"For the most part, yes. They loved each other very much."

Peter smiled. "I'm glad. She deserved to be loved. I wish I'd had more time with her."

Alex felt a tightness in his throat and choked back tears. "As do I. She… she died in my arms."

Peter was speechless for a few moments, stunned. "I apologize for reviving what must surely be a most poignant memory for you."

Alex nodded, composing himself.

"I loved her very much, as she did me. My father never could love her. I don't know why."

"I've met him, you know."

"*What?*"

Alex told him about the time Levine had come into the shop.

Peter sighed. "He has the occasional fit of temper. I know he loves me but sometimes he would get a strange look in his eyes and say that I looked too much like Mama." Peter laughed sadly. "Papa became more irritable as the money started running out and he had to sell off the plantation. Then he had to swallow his pride and run other people's farms for money. He hired out his slaves to them but finally had to sell them too. He became an overseer and was whipping the slaves out in the cane fields."

Alex had no problem imagining that.

"And then he divorced Mama and married again and started having children with his new wife, two boys and a girl."

"Did you like your stepmother?"

"I know it is unkind of me to say so, but to be honest, no. She was a common woman. Quite rude manners. Not at all like Mama. We moved to Fredericksted and Papa dabbled in real estate. Unsuccessfully. A friend of mine, Captain Samuel Grove of Charles Town, South Carolina, asked me to partner with him as a merchant in Beaufort. We have been quite successful. I have continued to write to my father and some friends. Papa ended up working as a janitor at a hospital. His little ones got sick and died. Then my stepmother died a month before Mama. I would move here to be with him were it not for my responsibilities in Beaufort."

"How tragic for your father."

"I have sent him money when he writes me expressing a need of it. But what of *your* father? Why are you not living with him?"

Alex informed him of James' impoverished financial situation.

Peter nodded, sympathetically. "I understand. Well…. before I return to South Carolina, I would very much like to see Mama's grave."

"I will show you. She is buried at The Grange."

"I do not wish to offend you, but I would prefer to be alone when I go. I know the way."

"I understand. I am not offended, brother."

Peter stood. "It has been a pleasure to meet you, Alexander. I wish you well."

"Likewise, Peter." They bowed. Peter placed a hand on Alex's shoulder and patted it warmly before turning to leave. Alex smiled, sadly.

1769 gave way to 1770. Another birthday came and went. Another year on the island.

Chapter Fourteen: The Girls

One day, Alex almost stumbled in his steps as he passed a familiar face out on the street. She was a few years older than the last time he'd seen her, and far more attractive than before: *Sally*. She was walking with her mother. Fortunately, her brother was nowhere to be seen.

Alex bowed politely to her and she stopped. Her mama, after advancing a few steps, looked back, and stopped as well. "Sally, how lovely it is to see you again."

"And you, Alex," she replied.

Her mother frowned. "Sally, darling, who is this young man you are speaking with so familiarly?"

"Oh, Mama, this is Alex Hamilton. An old friend of mine."

He smiled. She still considered him a friend.

"What have you been doing lately, Alex?"

"Working, mostly. My mother died."

She put a hand on his shoulder. "Oh, Alex, I'm so sorry to hear that."

"Thank you."

"We should catch up some day," she said.

"I would like that. Very much."

She leaned in and quickly whispered, "Sunday afternoon."

He nodded.

"Come along, Sally," her mother said. "Don't be rude."

She waved to him as she walked away, and he waved back. The rest of the day, he felt like he was walking on a cloud.

On Sunday, Alex went to Sally's backyard and she was out there, tending to the flower garden.

"Alex!" she cried upon seeing him. She opened her arms wide and he joined her happily in an embrace. "I have missed you so!" She grabbed his arm, gently, and looked around cautiously. "Come with me."

They headed into the nearby woods.

"Your brother, he—" began Alex.

"Is off at college. We won't be bothered by him again."

Alex smiled. "Good."

"I just don't want my parents to see you here. They'll get suspicious."

They talked and talked and talked some more. He told her about his job and his mother's death. About moving in with his cousin, uncle, and the Stevenses. She told him stories as well. She had a governess who had taught her to read and write. She also had a dancing master who taught her how to dance. She did a few steps with him. He had learned a little dancing from his mother and father when he had been younger, but he much preferred dancing with Sally. It had been a long time since he had done it, but he soon had mastered the skill well enough, as he continued seeing her every Sunday. The times when their bodies came close were the best and when she held his hands in hers.

They were sitting under a tree one day, leaning against each other, and Sally said, "Alex, I've been meaning to tell you something, but I'm not sure how."

"Yes?"

"I think I'm having certain kinds of feelings for you. Feelings I've never had for anyone else before."

"You do?" His heart leapt. He had seen her look at him a certain way, similar to how his mother had looked at his father at times. "I think I may have the same feelings for you."

"Truly?"

He nodded, looking deeply into her eyes. "You're beautiful."

Her eyes lit up even more than usual. "You think so?"

"Oh, yes," he said and began to stroke her hair with one hand. He placed the other hand on the side of her face. They leaned in closer to each other. Their lips met. Alex began to suck, gently, and she did likewise. They broke off. Smiling, they looked at each other.

"That was nice," she said.

"More than just nice," he said.

"Will you do it again?"

"Gladly."

They continued to explore each other's mouths. Alex enjoyed the warm feeling of her wrapped in his arms.

In the weeks that followed, they continued as usual, but with the addition of kissing every time they met. And then, kissing led to some further exploration of each other.

Alex tried his best to concentrate on work, but he started to make minor errors or to drift off with thoughts of Sally and become distracted. People at work started to take notice. One day, Cruger went to Alex's desk and expressed his concerns over the matter and asked Alex what was going on.

Alex blushed and said, nervously, "I-I-I have a… a girl."

"Ohhh…!" said Cruger, understanding dawning in his eyes. "Your first girlfriend. I get it, now, Alex. I'll never forget my first. But please try harder to focus on your work."

"I will, sir."

Cruger laughed for a moment, then apologized. "Sorry, Alex, but it makes me happy to know you are becoming a young man."

"Yes, sir." He went back to work.

Other employees had overheard the end of the conversation. From that time on, Alex was nicknamed "Cruger's Young Man."

Sally was a couple years older than Alex and at a marriageable age, although at the younger end of that spectrum. She was only a year younger than Alex's mother had been when she had wed Levine, in fact.

One day, Alex and Sally let things go more than a little too far and could not stop themselves. It was a little awkward, Alex had to admit, and it wasn't long before he was finished. Now, he realized, he had mixed feelings. He felt like he loved Sally. But he had taken from her that special gift that should be reserved for the marriage bed alone. He felt a little guilty.

When they got together the next Sunday, however, it was not their usual happy reunion. Distress showed clearly on Sally's face.

"What is it?" he asked. "What's wrong?"

She was shaking, red-faced, her eyes tearing. "My parents have arranged a marriage for me."

"What?" His heart sank.

"I'm afraid so."

"Forget that! I'll marry you!"

"I want to marry you too, but we *can't!"* She started to cry.

"Why not?" he asked. But he knew. He didn't want her to have to say it, so he did. "Because I'm too young and I'm a… penniless bastard?"

She nodded, sobbing.

He took her in his arms and comforted her. "I can't help being what I am. It's so unfair!"

"I can't see you anymore."

"Oh, Sally. Good God! How can I say goodbye to you? I love you!"

She kissed him, desperately. "I love you too! I'll never love anyone else!"

He looked her in the eyes and said, "Look at me." After a moment, she did. "You must try to love your betrothed." She shook her head, and he grabbed her shoulders. "Promise me you'll try to. And if you can't, at least try to live a happy life. I want you to. Please. Promise me." He wiped away her tears.

"I promise I'll try. If you will try to have a happy life, too, Alex."

"I will. I promise." He kissed her again and hugged her tightly. Then he released her. "Adieu, my darling Sally."

"Goodbye, my sweet Alex."

Sadly, he slowly walked away from her. When out of earshot and out of eyesight, he collapsed beneath a tree and sobbed. *Everyone I love is taken from me. God, why?*

"Your sandal is undone," Alex said to the girl. She had walked into the office of Kortright & Cruger with her father, who was discussing matters with Nicholas Cruger. Alex had seen the man before, but he had never seen this girl with him.

The girl bent over. She pulled back the hem of her floor-length dress, exposing a finely muscled calf and a slender ankle. Alex couldn't look away. He felt a stirring and suppressed it. His thoughts had been straying to Sally and how much he missed her. Maybe if he found another girl to love, it would ease the depression he felt. This girl was several years older than Alex, but about the same height. She was very beautiful, even more so than Sally, in a more sophisticated, cosmopolitan way. She was no innocent. He could tell. She was enticing him on purpose. It was working.

"Could you fasten it for me?" she

asked.

"Certainly," he replied.

She placed her leg on top of his thigh. His fingers shook slightly from nervousness as he fastened the buckle. The girl straightened and smiled at Alex. "Thank you," she said.

"My pleasure," said Alex, smiling back.

"I'm Coelia," she said. "Are you Alexander?"

He nodded. "You've heard of me?"

"You're becoming quite the famous young man, Alexander Hamilton, among those of us in the trade. I had to come and see you for myself. But no one said anything about how *cute* you are."

Now he knew she was flirting with him! Alex blushed. "I-I, uh…" Dammit, why did he have to stutter and be tongue-tied at a moment like this!

Coelia laughed softly. Was she laughing at him? But no, she strutted up to him with feline grace and put a hand on his shoulder. "I like you," she said. "Why don't you see me when you get off from work?"

"See you? Sure!" His voice broke on the last word. He'd picked a bad time to go through the changing of his voice.

She told him her address. He smelled her – the scent was intoxicating. "My papa is going away on a voyage. I'm staying home. There will only be a servant at home, and she drinks herself into a stupor every night…." She raised her eyebrows suggestively.

"Brilliant," said Alex. "I'll see you tonight."

"Mmmm. I'll look forward to it… Alexander." Her voice caressed his name.

The end of the shift couldn't come soon enough. Alex didn't stay for overtime that evening but headed with all speed to Coelia's address. It wasn't far. He would have time before he needed to be home and the Stevenses would surely assume he'd been working late as he often did.

He knocked on the door. Coelia opened it. She grabbed him and kissed him, slamming the door shut. Alex laughed with joy.

"Would you like some wine?"

He had tasted wine before, but just a sip here and there. He wanted to appear more experienced than he was. "I would love some."

She poured a glass of claret for him and one for herself. Alex sipped slowly at his, but Coelia quickly swallowed hers in three gulps. She poured another.

Alex increased the speed at which he drank, but still could not keep up with her. In all, he drank only two glasses to her four. When they were done, she took the glasses and put them down. She took Alex's hand and led him upstairs. She was giggling, but it may have been an affectation.

She pulled him into a bedroom. Coelia knew exactly what she was doing. She did things to him that Sally had never done. Things he had never even imagined before. She taught him much about how to please a woman.

Alex continued to see Coelia for several weeks. After the lessons of each evening, she would speak with him. At first, it was small talk. But, before long, she started to ask him questions about the business her father was doing with Kortright & Cruger.

The next time they met, Coelia gave Alexander more pleasure than ever. Afterward, during pillow talk, she said, "Do you have any sway with Nicholas Cruger?"

He shrugged. "Perhaps."

"Could you get my father a special deal on something? Just a little discount? For his repeat business? I mean, that's only fair, isn't it? You could drop a word in Cruger's ear." Her tone of voice was calculatingly nonchalant.

"I don't know."

"Try. Promise me that you'll try to. For me." Then she did something to him artfully contrived to convince him. "Just talk to him," she said when she was finished. "That's all."

"I reckon it wouldn't hurt to ask…"

Alex had said he'd ask, and he was a man of his word. As he had expected, however, Cruger said no.

Coelia was not very happy about this when Alex told her. She pouted for a time. The rest of that evening was not much fun.

The next time they met, she started asking him questions that were, at first, mildly general about the firm, but slowly approached more and more sensitive intelligence about its internal policies. Alex felt that he was getting dangerously close to revealing insider secrets that he really shouldn't tell her. Oh, but she was so… so *alluring* that he was tempted to tell her just a little something. But, then he thought, a little would lead to a little more, and then even more. He wanted to please her but, no, there were certain things he just could not bring himself to say. He refused to betray his employer.

"I really can't tell you that."

"Don't be silly. Of course, you can. What's it to you? It's just a stupid job you don't even like. You don't own the business.

They'll never know who told me this."

"No. I'm not going to say it."

She started to kiss him on his chest and moved lower. "Yes, you can. You want this, don't you? I'd do anything for you, Alexander—"

Despite the seductive way she'd said his name – a ploy that had almost worked on him before - he stopped her. "No!"

Now the smile was gone from her face. "Fine, then, forget it! Get dressed and leave! Don't come back until you're willing to be my friend." She started to cry, but he could tell the tears were fake.

As he was heading out, she said, "I don't get why you like Cruger better than me."

He turned around. "For one thing, Cruger is honest with me. He doesn't use me."

"Doesn't he?"

That hurt. There was just enough truth in her question to give him pause.

Sometimes, he did, in fact, feel like he had been used. He felt like he wasn't being paid enough and that he was cut out for more than just being a clerk. He felt that even if he had been a manager for the firm, it wouldn't have been enough. It wasn't what he really wanted in life. No, there was something else out there for him. He just wasn't quite sure what that was as of yet.

But, regardless of whether or not he was, in fact, being used by Cruger, he could not bring himself to betray the man. His parents had raised him to be a man of honor. Coelia be damned. That artful little slut. Alex stomped out of the house, angrily. Coelia followed, yelling after him. "You'll regret this, Alexander Hamilton! You'll miss this! You'll miss me! You'll come back with your tail between your legs, you little bastard!"

He stopped, clenched a fist in anger then sighed and released it. Despite being tempted, despite the fact that Coelia deserved it, he could never hit a female.

As soon as he arrived home he pulled out a piece of paper, a quill and inkpot. He needed a catharsis, and this was the way to get it. He wrote a poem about Coelia, painting her somewhat as a manipulative feline. She had always resembled a cat in her physical grace and the slyness of her personality.

> *Coelia's an artful little slut;*
> *Be fond, she'll kiss, et cetera—but*
> *She must have all her will;*
> *For, do but rub her 'gainst the grain*
> *Behold a storm, blow winds and rain,*
> *Go bid the waves be still.*
> *So, stroking puss's velvet paws*
> *How well the jade conceals her claws*
> *And purs; but if at last*
> *You hap to squeeze her somewhat hard,*
> *She spits—her back up—prenez garde;*
> *Good faith she has you fast.*

She had, indeed, held him fast for a time, but then she had pushed things too far. He had never loved her. He had found her very attractive and perhaps he would miss what they had done together. But he hadn't loved her like he had Sally. He never saw her again and he was glad of it.

He also wrote a poem that reminded

him of the sweet innocence of his Sally,
portraying her as a shepherdess:

In yonder mead my love I found
Beside a murm'ring brook reclin'd:
Her pretty lambkins dancing round
Secure in harmless bliss.
I bad the waters gently glide,
And vainly hush'd the heedless
wind,
Then, softly kneeling by her side,
I stole a silent kiss—
She wak'd, and rising sweetly
blush'd
By far more artless than the dove:
With eager haste I onward rush'd,
And clasp'd her in my arms;
Encircled thus in fond embrace
Our panting hearts beat mutual
love—
A rosy-red o'er spread her face
And brighten'd all her charms.
Silent she stood, and sigh'd consent
To every tender kiss I gave;
I closely urg'd—to church we went,
And hymen join'd our hands.
Ye swains behold my bliss complete;
No longer then your own delay;
Believe me love is doubly sweet
In wedlocks holy bands.—
Content we tend our flocks by day,
Each rural pleasures amply taste;
And at the suns retiring ray
Prepare for new delight:

When from the field we haste away,
And send our blithsome care to rest,
We fondly sport and fondly play,
And love away the night.

He sent both poems to the *Royal Danish American Gazette* to publish them. He didn't give them his full name, just his initials. That way, he could deny to Coelia or anyone else that he had been the author of the poems. To further confuse the question of his identity, he overstated his age. Alex felt justified in doing this since he was mature beyond his years. He had experienced more than most boys of his age, had taken on more responsibility than most boys of his age. Dammit, he *felt* like he was 17. He might as well claim it. He said a little prayer, asking God to forgive him for this little white lie.

They published the poems on April 6.

He hadn't changed Coelia's name on the draft he'd sent in. Now everyone would see her for the wanton little manipulator she was. *No one calls Alexander Hamilton a "bastard" and gets away with it,* thought Alex, with a vengeful smile on his face.

Chapter Fifteen: The Trip

Alex continued in his life as before, slightly older, but much wiser. He was now more on guard for people who would use him. He told Cruger about Coelia and what she had done. He left out the salacious details and merely said, suggestively, that they had struck up a "friendship of sorts."

Cruger raised an eyebrow. "Apparently her father targeted you and felt you'd be gullible because of your youth and susceptibility to his daughter's charms."

"I must admit, I was reeled in by her siren song, at first. But I saw the danger before I said anything to betray you."

"I appreciate this, Alex. You have no idea how much. I shall be on my guard in my dealing with her father in future. I hope the girl didn't hurt your feelings overmuch."

Alex shook his head. "I wasn't in love with her. I liked her, but I sensed there was something a little duplicitous about her."

"Find a good, honest woman to love. Like I did. Did you know?"

Alex shook his head. "No."

"I'm getting married."

"Congratulations, sir! To whom?

"Anna de Nully."

"The daughter of the town captain?"

"The very one."

"She's very beautiful."

"Hands off her, Alex." A teasing smile lit up his face.

Alex laughed. "I wouldn't think of it, sir."

Alex devoted himself even more to his job in the months that followed. Cruger continued to test the young man's abilities to lead. He showed him more and more of the business, focusing on administration of the office and its personnel. Was he preparing Alex for a promotion? He certainly hoped so.

Cruger took Alex with him every time he boarded a ship to inspect its cargo. Cruger would look at the ship's cargo manifest and show it to Alex. It listed what was contained in each numbered parcel. It also listed the destination of each one. On one particular occasion, Cruger pointed at the crates and barrels and criticized the order in which they had been stowed. He handed the manifest to Alex. "Notice how some of the parcels that are to be offloaded here in St. Croix are stored below or behind others that are destined for other ports the ship will arrive at in future?"

Alex checked the list and saw that it was so. "Yes, Mr. Cruger. Why would they do it this way?"

Cruger narrowed his eyes. "Carelessness on part of those who loaded things? Lack of supervision? Too liberal partaking of the grog? All of these and other reasons as well, perhaps." He shook his head. "It's a shame. It will take longer to unload things and cause costly delays in the ship's schedule. Also, take note of how scattered about the crates are. There is no logical sense to any of it. It is all… hickledy-pickledy. You see that, yes?"

"Indeed, I do, sir. Hickledy-pickledy." He shook his head. "Grog."

Cruger nodded. "Grog," he concurred. They looked at each other and laughed.

Cruger had the crew open the parcels so that Alex and he could examine the contents. "Do you see, Alex," Cruger said, "how this flour looks darker than usual?"

"Yes, sir."

"That means it's stale. I wonder how long it was sitting in storage before they shipped it. Or perhaps it has made the rounds without being sold for whatever reason, glutted markets and the like." Cruger shook his head. "It's no good for anything now but slave food. I must now negotiate a discount of the purchasing price."

Alex felt it was grossly unfair that the lowest quality of edible commodities be reserved solely for the most abused, most disadvantaged, and hardest-working people in the islands. But he judiciously kept his mouth shut over such things. It did him no good to protest. Perhaps, he hoped, there would come a time and a place in which he could encourage others to change this inequitable and inhumane state of affairs. But that time and place were not now and not here.

"That's a shame, sir."

Cruger shrugged. "That's the shipping business. Things don't always go to plan."

In addition to these educational excursions, Cruger loaned Alex a few useful books. One large volume in particular appealed to Hamilton: Malachy Postlethwayt's *The Universal Dictionary of Trade and Commerce.* Alex read this and the other books with his typically voracious appetite for the written word. The business was now becoming his whole world, his singular focus. *The projector is constant,* he thought, recalling the letter he had written Ned Stevens. *Indeed, mon frère, I am constant. As are you, no doubt.* But he had little time to think of Ned and his life far, far away. And even less time to write him.

Alex grew in competence and he felt confident that he could do whatever Cruger assigned him to do. He couldn't help but notice, however, that his boss seemed to look a bit more tired than usual. He seemed paler than was natural and there were dark rings under his eyes. Alex also caught the man occasionally wincing and grasping at his abdomen in pain. He was concerned. Cruger, though more than ten years Alex's senior, was still a young man, in the prime of his life. He shouldn't be having any serious health problems, but the signs were there. Alex wished he knew more about medicine and could help.

"Alex, could you please come into my office?" he asked Alex one day in late September.

"Of course, Mr. Cruger."

Alex sat in a chair and Cruger closed the door then sat behind his desk.

"This conversation must be kept in the strictest confidence, Alex. I feel I can trust you as a man of honor to keep your word not to speak of it outside this room."

"I won't tell anyone, sir. I promise."

"Very well, then. I have, for some months now, been experiencing pains in my gut. I don't know what is wrong with me and I have consulted several doctors here in the islands. No one has been able to give me any sort of relief. All they do is bleed me, which only makes weaker. I don't think they are as good as the physicians I used to see when I was living in New York. And so, I have decided, for the sake of my health, I must take a temporary leave of absence to go there for a proper diagnosis and treatment."

"That certainly seems to be your only option at the present time."

"And I must therefore place someone I trust in charge of this office, someone I feel is a competent leader. I can think of no one who can do that but you."

"I, sir?"

"Yes. Have you wondered why I have been instructing you and testing you?"

"I thought perhaps you were priming me for a promotion."

"In a manner of speaking, yes,

although merely a temporary one for now. In future, perhaps, it will become more permanent. I would like to move back to New York someday and will need to find someone to run the business here. I don't know if that interests you as of yet, but perhaps if you give this a test run and find that you enjoy the work, we can discuss any future plans upon my return."

Alex nodded. "Very well, sir. You can certainly count on me to do the job to the best of my ability. I am, however, concerned for how they will perceive me, my youth—"

"You know the employees here will respect your orders."

"Most of them, perhaps, but I will also have to give orders to ships' captains and the like."

"As to that, I will have a power of attorney drafted for you and a notarized statement that I am granting you my full authority to act on my behalf. You won't have to get my permission beforehand on any decision, including that of firing any employee found to be guilty of a terminable offense. I will specify all of this in the document, of course. So, do you accept?"

"I do, sir."

Cruger smiled. "You don't know how much of a relief that is to me."

"When are you leaving?"

"In a week. I have matters I must personally attend to first. I also want to give you enough time to prepare yourself and for you and the rest of the staff to get used to your being in this position of authority before I leave."

Cruger made the announcement to the rest of the staff. He did not tell them that the trip to New York was for medical reasons, although certainly, the man's pallor was noticeable, and the staff suspected such was the cause for his departure. Most of the staff were indeed friendly to Alex, having known him well for years, and accepted his authority without question or envy – at least so it appeared.

Chapter Sixteen: The Boss

On October 15, Cruger boarded a ship. Alex felt a weight descend upon his shoulders. Perhaps the stress of it all caused him to start feeling unwell himself a couple of weeks into his new position. He soldiered on through the headaches, the heart palpitations, and the occasional bout of vomiting. Perhaps it was just nerves. He worked as hard as he could bear, assigning tasks to others as much as possible. Fortunately, he quickly recovered from the illness and was able to continue his duties without pause. He was adjusting to the role and felt more comfortable in it as time passed. He wrote letters to Cruger, keeping him apprised of the goings-on in the business.

Sometimes he had to address a problem with a shipment. Stale flour arrived from Philadelphia, which was darker than usual in appearance, darker even than the shipment Cruger had shown Alex before; it even had worms in it. Of course, Alex negotiated the selling price considerably downward before issuing the payment to the seller.

He also had some trouble with Captain William Newton, a relatively inexperienced captain who had been put in command of the sloop named *Thunderbolt* that was jointly owned by Nicholas Cruger, Jacob Walton, and John Harris, in an equal partnership. In Alex's opinion, the ship needed guns for its defense from pirates and from the Spanish Coast Guard. Unfortunately, none were to be found in all of St. Croix. On November 16, Hamilton wrote Cruger's brother Tileman, who ran the Curaçao office, to help Newton arm the ship. It was not done. On the same day, he instructed the captain to get a cargo of as many mules as he could fit in the hold along with sufficient feed for them, and to hurry back as the harvest would come early that year and the mules were needed to assist with it.

Tileman had some staves which Hamilton knew would sell for a higher price on St. Croix, so he asked him to send them in the *Thunderbolt*. Tileman did so. The sloop arrived back at St. Croix on the 27th with the staves and some other items. It then departed for the American continent. In

December, Alex received some welcome news from Cruger that his health was improving.

As January was wearing on, Alex started to grow concerned as the *Thunderbolt* had been expected back and, thus far, had failed to return. He feared misadventure. Any number of things could have happened. Pirates, storms, fires. Possibly even a mutiny. He received word from Tileman Cruger that he hadn't, in fact, armed the ship because his brother hadn't told him to. Alex was furious. Didn't he trust that Nicholas had given him complete authority over the enterprise? That included the sloop!

Other ships were arriving at the port and Alex spoke with their captains. They apprised him of delays due to doldrums, and that the only winds they were getting were blowing in the wrong direction. Alex felt a preliminary sense of possible relief. Maybe that was why the *Thunderbolt*'s arrival was delayed. At least, that was what he hoped and prayed.

January was almost at an end when the *Thunderbolt* finally returned to St. Croix.

Alex had never been happier to see any ship before in his life. He ran to the sloop when he saw it ease into the dock. Of course, there was no sign of any guns anywhere on it. He boarded the ship.

Captain Newton, standing on the deck, greeted him. "Mr. Hamilton!" he said.

"Captain Newton! I cannot tell you how relieved I am to see you. I feared the worst until I started to hear reports of contrary winds."

"Indeed. The voyage took far longer than usual, as a consequence."

"Let us waste no time, then. Show me the cargo." The captain began to lead Alex below. As they walked, the youth said, "I am especially interested in the mules you took possession of. How many did you acquire?"

"Forty-eight." He opened the hold that housed the beasts. Alex was immediately assaulted with a foul smell, not just of the expected animal waste, but of a rotten meat smell. What he saw next was even more stunning.

No grass remained for the poor animals to eat. Many were lying down. Ribs stood out all too clearly from their emaciated bodies.

Alex cried out in shock. "Good God! Did you store no grass for them?"

"Of course, I did!" said Newton, defensively. "I stored enough for a regular trip. This one just took a bit longer. I didn't expect that to happen."

Alex shook his head. "Things don't always go to plan on the open sea. You should have stowed extra on board just in case."

"I will do so in future," the captain replied, slightly sheepishly.

"See that you do. Very well then." Alex entered the hold to examine the mules. Seven were dead. He thought for a moment, then turned to Newton. "Have your men dispose of the dead ones. The rest they will lead to a pasture I know of at Number 33 and I will contract with the owner to have them pastured as long as it takes for them to restore their health." He shook his head. "What a shame. We could have gotten 40 pounds sterling for this lot! Now…." He did some calculations in his head. "We'd be lucky to get 75 pieces of eight each. After pasturing, however, perhaps… 100, and I fear we shall lose more of them, perhaps even a full third of them. Cruger and the other owners won't be pleased. You know, I will have to report this."

"I realize that, sir," said Newton, looking downcast.

"Next time, do you think you could fit 60 mules in there? Those who know how to judge these matters have said so to me."

"Oh, I doubt that, Mr. Hamilton. I believe 48 would be the highest number we could possibly accommodate."

"Hmm. I'll broach this subject with Tileman and see what he has to say."

"As to him, believe me, I urged him to arm the ship, but he wouldn't."

"I'm aware of that, Captain. I am none too pleased with him over this issue. Next time, if Tileman refuses again, you rent the guns yourself. We will reimburse you for the expense. It shouldn't be more than 10 pieces of eight per month for two guns. You can do that, yes?"

"Yes, Mr. Hamilton."

"I must now go to the pasture and make arrangements. I shall return to inspect the remainder of the cargo. As soon as we remove it and load what we have here for you, you'll need to embark for Curaçao with all due speed. We will speak again, Captain." He gave the man a firm look. "Your servant, sir."

The captain tipped his hat to Alex. "Yours, Mr. Hamilton."

The months continued to tick by slowly. Alex stepped aboard *The Lightbourne*, commanded by Captain Gibbs. He shook his head as he examined the cargo, manifest in hand.

"What is the matter?" asked Gibbs.

"What is the *matter?*" Alex echoed, incredulous. "Don't you see how scattered about your cargo is stored, Captain? It's all hickledy-pickledy! It will delay the unloading process and put you even further behind schedule. Well… let's take a look." He stepped up to a crate that held mahogany lumber. The crate looked like it hadn't been sealed properly and Alex feared the worst. He had the men open it. Looking inside, he saw his fears confirmed. "Look at this!" he said to the captain. "It's all waterlogged. It's useless for anything but end work." He shook his head. "We will have to reduce the price by three-fourths."

"You're jesting, Mr. Hamilton."

"This is no laughing matter. We have little demand at this time for lumber of this… *quality.* It will be difficult for us to sell it even at this reduced price. What I am offering you is more than fair."

"But—"

"Take it or leave it."

Gibbs scratched his head, discouraged. He had little choice but to accept the offer. "Aye. Perhaps you're right."

"In future, for pity's sake, make sure the crates are properly sealed. This is on you, Captain Gibbs!"

Fortunately, the rest of the cargo was in a much better condition.

It seemed to Alex that the job entailed little more than dealing with problem after problem and was not exactly an enjoyable occupation. Clearly, running an international trading firm was not his life's calling. And yet, what else was there for him? A war? Perhaps, ultimately, that would be his destiny. But he would ponder that later. For now, he had too much to deal with.

To compound the problems involved with the shipping business itself, there was a scarcity of money to go around. Without money, Alex thought, person A doesn't pay person B what he owes him. And because person B owes person C, who owes person D, and so on, no one receives the money they are due. Without a swift flow of money, the economy slows, and the people suffer. The issuance of paper money would solve the problem of a scarcity of specie. Of course, as he had learned from his studies, there were inherent dangers with the use of paper money, such as the runaway inflation that would result from the overprinting of money. With proper regulation and management of the same, the system could work, and in fact had worked in various places in the past.

Alex sat at the desk in Cruger's office examining expense reports when he started to notice a disturbing trend. Something was not quite adding up with the invoices submitted from the firm's attorney, Gerhard Hassell. Clearly, the man had been overcharging the firm for a considerable time. How had Cruger failed to see this? Had he just trusted the man and not taken a look at his ledgers? He called Hassell into the office and went over the account book with him.

"Please explain to me, sir, how you calculated this figure, and all of the others for the last three months."

Hassell folded his arms, his expression haughty. "I don't have to explain anything to you, boy."

Alex stared at him, a firm look on his face, for several long moments. No one else had treated him with such disrespect. Hassell stared back, his expression unchanged. When the stare-down didn't work, Alex said, "Yes, you do. I am acting in the interest of our employer, Mr. Nicholas Cruger."

"I will explain things to Cruger if he ever asks me. I doubt he will, however. He's never expressed any dissatisfaction with the job I've done for him."

Alex stood, his anger starting to boil to the surface at the man's insubordination. "You will justify your expenses, mister, or you are terminated."

Hassell laughed. "You can't fire me. You have no authority."

"I have his power of attorney. You should know—"

"Yes, yes, yes. I drafted it myself." Nonchalantly, he lounged back in his chair and examined his fingernails. "But Cruger only did that to humor you and get you to do the job."

"It is legally binding."

Hassell waved his hand, dismissively, a smug grin on his face. "What are you going to do about it?"

Alex started writing an order that

fired Hassell. "You are to vacate these premises by the close of business today and leave all items belonging to the firm, or I will call the constables and have you arrested."

"Very funny, kid."

Alex stared at him, his expression even more fierce than before. "Are you going to do what I say?"

Now Hassell was starting to get angry himself. He had expected the diminutive youth to give in and let him go about his business. He hadn't expected this fortitude in one so young. He stood up. "No."

Alex exited the room, Hassell followed. In the middle of the office, Alex cleared his throat and spoke loudly enough so that everyone could hear him. "May I have everyone's attention, please! Mr. Hassell's employment here has been terminated. He requires assistance to clear out his desk. Do I have any volunteers?"

Several employees raised their hands. Hassell had never been very popular.

"Thank you. Go to it, men."

Despite Hassell's loud and very vocal protests, the desk was quickly cleared of all his personal effects. He started to threaten anyone who dared touch his possessions.

"Please, Mr. Hassell," Alex said, a smug grin on his face. "Do not make any further threats of violence. Do not force me to call the constables. They are not the gentle sort."

"Cruger will not stand for this!" Hassell said. "He needs me. You'll be fired for this, Hamilton!"

"There are other attorneys on this island. Perhaps he'll have one of them sue you. And he may even have you arrested for embezzlement. Now, will you kindly vacate the premises, *sir*?"

Red-faced with fury, Hassell picked up the box of his belongings and headed for the door. At the threshold, he turned around. "You haven't heard the last of this!" were his parting words.

When the door closed, the office

burst into applause. Several employees clapped Alex on the back and congratulated him on the good job he had just done.

"Don't celebrate too much, lads," Alex said. "I now have to hire a new attorney." Before long, he had hired a man named Hans Buus. He wrote Cruger regarding this affair and included copies of Hassell's ledgers. Cruger wrote back that he had been unaware of the deception his attorney had been perpetrating and thanked Alex for his diligence. He approved of the new attorney.

Chapter Seventeen: The Reverend

In late February, Hamilton received a letter from Nicholas Cruger which stated that his health had improved sufficiently to allow his return. His ship would arrive in mid-March. On the 17th, Cruger set foot once again on the island. The office was jubilant and threw a party to welcome back their leader. Although he was still a little weak, Cruger's color had returned and he was infused with a joy in his face that Alex had never seen before. The youth was relieved. He felt as if a large weight had been lifted from his shoulders.

Many of the employees, Alex included, attended Cruger's wedding to Anna de Nully on April 15. The ceremony was held at the captain's house. They watched as the beautiful, blushing bride walked down the aisle on the arm of her father, Town Captain Bertram Pieter de Nully. The minister who officiated the wedding was named Hugh Knox.

After the ceremony, they attended the reception. Alex was sitting at a table with several other employees when Reverend Knox asked if a vacant chair was available and if they wouldn't mind him sitting there. They welcome the reverend. The man regaled them with a very sincere smile, which he almost constantly displayed. They exchanged the usual pleasantries, the young men all introducing themselves to Knox and vice versa. "You…" said Knox, "you are young Alexander Hamilton?"

"You've heard of me?" Alex asked.

"Oh, yes! Nick was raving about you, calling you his 'Young Man.' Is it true that you actually ran the office for five months?"

The other employees rolled their eyes good-naturedly. How many times would they have to hear this story?

"Yes."

Knox shook his head with incredulous admiration. "How old are you, if you don't mind me asking?"

"Fifteen, Reverend."

"Fifteen. And is it true that you fired

the attorney?"

Alex confirmed it. He and the other employees told Knox the story, as well as the debacle involving the starved mules.

"What about you?" Alex asked. "I've never seen you before. Have you recently arrived in Christiansted?"

"Yes. I had a church before on the island of Saba for seventeen years. My father-in-law is the governor of that island. I came here, well, for more money and a better opportunity."

"Your accent is… I can't quite place it. It sounds a little Scottish, but…"

"I'm originally from Ireland but was educated in my father's native Scotland. Then, I furthered my education at Yale College in Connecticut."

Alex brightened up at this. "You studied on the mainland?" he asked, with great interest.

"Yes. Divinity and medicine. I attended the College of New Jersey in Princeton for my post-graduate studies. I learned from one of its founders, Reverend

Aaron Burr." His face darkened.

"What is it?"

"He died. About fifteen years ago." Knox sighed. He raised a glass. "To absent friends."

They all joined in the toast. Hamilton had his own toast. "To our lost loved ones."

After drinking, Knox said, "But this is a wedding. It should be a joyful occasion, my friends!"

Alex's lips twitched upward slightly. "Yes. So, are you a physician?"

"Yes, which makes me doubly useful, I reckon. Saving men's souls as well as their bodies."

"My grandfather was a physician. And my best friend Ned Stevens is attending Kings College in New York, studying medicine. I am very interested in the subject, myself, but…"

"But…?"

Alex blushed. "I have no means to go."

Knox was silent for a moment. "I am aware of your predicament, son. Nick told me much about your situation."

Alex wondered how much Knox knew about him. Did he know that Alex was a bastard?

"Trust in the Lord," said Knox. "Hope in the Lord, who will surely be thy deliverance. There is no predestiny. Our lives are shaped by our choices and our efforts. As long as we follow the Good Lord's commandments, He will bless our efforts. Have you all heard of the Great Awakening?"

They nodded.

"That is what I am here to preach. You are all welcome to attend my Sunday services, starting next month." He told them where and when they would be held. "We are building a new church, but until it is completed, we must meet elsewhere."

"I shall certainly endeavor my utmost to attend that which, no doubt, will be a most inspirational service," said Alex.

"Nick told me you have quite the way

with words. I am delighted to see he was not at all exaggerating."

Alex smiled, blushing modestly. "Thank you, Reverend, for your kind words."

Alex was true to his word. The next Sunday, he sat in the pew, mesmerized by Knox's fiery oratory. His voice was loud and clear, his words eloquent. It was an inspiring mixture of the revolutionary new doctrine of free will versus the Puritanical notion of predestination and it greatly appealed to Hamilton, who wanted to believe that he controlled his own destiny. He felt hope stirring in his heart.

He attended Knox's services every Sunday from that time on.

At times, he felt like Knox was speaking directly to him. One particular Sunday in August, as he sat in a pew near the altar of the newly constructed church, he noticed Knox's eyes often connecting with his own.

"God is an infinite, incomprehensible being," Knox said, "a boundless, bottomless ocean of perfection; and many things in his nature still remain profound and unsearchable mysteries to our natural reason. Let us suppose that instead of giving us a revelation, our religion had cast an impenetrable veil over the life to come and the future slate of rewards and punishments that it contains. Would we renounce fleshly and sinful lusts solely because they are unmanly, unbecoming and greatly prejudicial to the present interests of society and individuals? Men who are willing to forget the present satisfactions arising from virtue for the gratification of their passions and appetites would freely indulge them, having no future punishment to fear."

Alex thought back on his life thus far, and in particular on his encounters with Sally and Coelia. He *hadn't* been thinking about Heaven and Hell when he had been with them. He had found a slice of Heaven with Sally, and, in a way, with Coelia as well. But the feelings were transitory, earthly. Now, his thoughts were turning toward the hereafter.

Knox continued. "Youth is an age of inexperience and therefore needs a guide. Young, undisciplined minds have in them a kind of natural impetuosity which renders them averse to deliberation and impatient of delay. Hence it is that we find them so often making wrong and false judgments. It's true indeed that, when a proposition lies before the mind, the terms of which are in any measure understood, the mind cannot well restrain itself from forming some judgment about its truth or falsehood. It may and ought to reserve a place for a future judgment upon further knowledge and clearer evidence."

That is true, Alex thought. He called to mind the many times he'd made snap judgments. Maybe he should deliberate a bit more in the future, gather facts and analyze them before drawing conclusions.

"The period of infancy and childhood are wholly sensual; our bodily senses and appetites are our first masters and instructors for the first 10 or 12 years of life. From our very cradles we are witnesses of the vices and irregularities of our parents and others around us and therefore can hardly believe them to be serious when they dissuade us from those very vices which they themselves practice."

His parents had, in essence, been adulterers. They had told him about their church wedding. But was it really appropriate for them to have done that, his mother not being legally free to remarry? And had she not erred greatly in marrying Levine to begin with? Shouldn't she have waited until she could have been better acquainted with him and could make a more informed decision about his character? Or had she married him purely out of desperation to secure her inheritance from her father as she had once told Alex?

"The youth is sent abroad into a corrupt and ensnaring world with a few abstruse definitions of religion floating in his memory. He will feel the opposition is so strong between the natural dispositions of his own heart and the pure and holy precepts of the Christian religion that he will begin to wish that Christianity were false. He will find the writings of infidels so agreeable to his own wishes and so indulgent to his vices that henceforth he will renounce his religion."

Alex resolved that he would not let that happen to him. He was on the verge of manhood and he must guard himself, for he knew his own drives were all too powerful. Was it this way for all young men? Perhaps not to the same degree as it was for him. At least, he hoped not or surely all of mankind was doomed to wage a perpetual war against their own licentiousness. Had his precocious sexual experiences contributed to the strength of his present urges? He still felt them whenever he saw a beautiful young lady look at him with unfeigned interest. That happened a little too often. Alex had noticed that his face was taking on a more mature quality that enhanced his attractiveness. He had been shaving for a couple years and the whiskery shadow on his chin and upper lip gave him a masculine look that hadn't been there in his prepubescent years.

The reverend concluded his sermon with advice Alex took to heart: "Let us instead make the word of God our daily counselor, read with our own eyes and judge with our own understandings. God's word shall preserve us from being tossed to and fro and carried about with every wind of doctrine by the light of corrupt men. A soul thus furnished can never be at a loss to overcome the wicked one and repel all his fiery darts. Man was created upright but he fell by the abuse of his own liberty. Weakness and corruption were unavoidably conveyed to his posterity, which involves us in vice and misery through no personal fault of our own. Our own ignorance and meekness keep us in a dependence on the illuminating spirit of God for direction into all necessary truth. We long for that bright and refulgent day when the veil of ignorance shall be taken from our minds. As the glimmering light of a candle to that of open day, or as the pale and feeble rays of the moon to the effulgent brightness of the sun in its meridian splendor, such was the light of former dispensations when compared with the marvelous light which the glorious gospel has shed upon a benighted world."

A benighted world, indeed, one which Alex must make his way through. Alone.

A mere clerk again, Alex was back to work as usual at the office of Kortright & Cruger. One day seemed like just another day, but on that day he saw something he found rather odd. Reverend Hugh Knox walked in through the front door. He caught Alex's eye and nodded at him. Alex nodded back. But Knox didn't approach Alex. Rather, he greeted Nicholas Cruger, who escorted him into his office and closed the door. Alex wondered what was going on. Did Cruger have need of spiritual counseling? If so, about what? No, it wasn't anything like that. Somehow, Hamilton *knew* it had something to do with *himself.*

Although he had no clue as to what, exactly, that could be. After about half an hour, the door opened, and Knox came out. He shook Cruger's hand and headed over to Alex. He was holding a book.

"This was one of the books I studied while in college. I don't have need to for it, anymore, but you do." He held out a medical textbook.

Alex took it. "You didn't have to do this for me," he said, wonder in his voice at the man's kindness and generosity.

"Nonsense. A young mind such as yours should never go to waste. Read, young Alex."

"Thank you."

Knox continued to speak with Alex after every church service and occasionally visited at the office. Alex couldn't help but like the man and felt completely at ease around him. He wasn't like other holier-than-thou preachers Alex had encountered, some of whom had looked down their noses at Hamilton and his parents because of his illegitimacy. In time, as he became better acquainted with the reverend, he found that

Knox held him blameless for the stain upon his birth. Alex was also delighted to find that Knox shared his views on slavery and believed in the equality of the races. He owned thirteen slaves himself, but, like Hamilton's parents, he treated them well, and like Alex himself, had taught them how to read and write.

Knox and his family welcomed Alex into his home to peruse his library and borrow books. He had a wealth of subjects there, and, of course, had more books on divinity than the Stevenses had. Alex had never particularly been a religious devotee, but he was finding himself praying fervently more and more often - daily, in fact - and reading the Bible with a voracity he had never experienced before.

The next chance he had to speak with Cruger, he brought the subject up of the reverend's meetings with his boss. Cruger replied cryptically. "You are cut out for more than this, Alex. I can tell. The way you handled Hassell and those captains while I was gone - men far older than you – was most impressive. You have courage and leadership skills. I know you will go far in future in whatever profession you choose to pursue."

"I certainly hope to, sir," said Alex, "but what—"

"You will know when the time has come."

"But sir—"

"You have work to do, don't you?"

"Yes, sir. I—"

"Don't worry, Alex. Things are looking up for you. Good things await you." He patted Alex on the shoulder warmly and went back to his office.

Good things, Alex thought. He heard nothing else of the matter. Time passed; it was now the end of August.

Chapter Eighteen: The Hurricane

On Monday, August 31, Alex worked a full day, then set out for the Stevens' house as usual. A moderate wind was blowing, and the sky was very dark, overcast with swirling clouds. Filled with the usual sense of alarm that always overcame him upon seeing a hurricane approaching, he quickened his pace. The wind quickly grew in intensity, and little Alex was afraid it might blow him away. He struggled, grabbing onto fences, railings, anything to help him get back home. Rain began to fall in sheets. Mrs. Stevens was looking out the window as he approached, her face a mask of worry. She opened the door with difficulty and pulled him in.

"Hurricane!" he cried.

"Yes, I know. And Thomas isn't home yet."

They stared out the window. The Stevens children and the slaves joined them, apprehension clear on their faces. One minute. Two minutes. A feeling of dread gripped Alex's heart. At last, they saw a figure approaching. Much to their relief, it was Mr. Stevens. They pulled him in and immediately proceeded to bar the windows. They hunkered down in the center of the house where it was safer.   Alex could see out of a window. The group held onto each other for hours.

Finally, the wind died down for a time, but they all knew it was just the eye of the storm. The wind would soon be back, and worse than before. They stepped outside with lanterns to view the damage. It was too dark to see much, but what they could see nearby told much. Fallen tree limbs lay strewn about everywhere. The surrounding structures were still standing, though perhaps a little damaged. They took what time they had to reinforce their defenses and board up the windows. After about an hour, the wind started up again.

Alex had been through hurricanes before, but this was far beyond anything he had ever experienced. He saw flashes of light, but they weren't just lightning. He could see balls of fire flying through the sky. The wind was howling so loudly that he had to put his hands over his ears. He heard a dreadful crashing sound – had a nearby house just been destroyed? Outside, neighbors were screaming; Hamilton would never forget those sounds of terror. Shaking with fear, he prayed for the poor, unfortunate souls those voices belonged to. He also prayed for himself and the Stevens family. *God, please save us. God, please hold this house together.* He could feel the house, sturdy as it was, shaking from the buffeting of the wind. Debris pummeled the roof with loud bangs. One of the Stevens kids whimpered – he wasn't sure which one. He put a reassuring hand out to touch what he believed was the shoulder of the child.

From above them came an awful crashing sound and they covered their heads as part of the roof crashed down upon them. The children screamed. Rain started to come in and they moved away from the huge hole in the roof. Thomas Stevens started to pray out loud and everyone joined in with him. They held on to each other during the rest of the terrible storm.

Time broke down to seconds. Alex feared each moment would be his last. He knew the others felt the same. He hated feeling so helpless. They were in God's hands. Perhaps the Lord would be merciful. He could do nothing but pray and hope, pray and hope, hope and pray….

At last, it seemed the wind was dying down. Was it? Yes! It was! They were spared. The whole family cheered, hugging and kissing each other, Alex included. After a time, dawn began to light the sky and they ventured outside.

Alex had never seen such devastation. The buildings all around him weren't just damaged, they were razed to the ground. Debris covered the ground in all directions. Ships, driven to ground by the wind, were damaged beyond any hope of repair. People wandered the streets, crying, begging, calling out for lost family members.

They examined the extensive damage to the Stevens home. In addition to the holes in the roof, the glass windows had been shattered. The outbuildings were gone. A tree had crashed into the side of the house, causing a large, gaping breach in the wall. Repairing the damage would take weeks, if not months, of work and would cost a small fortune. Fortunately, Mr. Stevens was wealthy enough to afford it. But what about those poor unfortunates who could not afford to repair their own homes?

Rescue efforts were quickly underway, and a community meeting was called on Sunday. Many of the prominent citizens who could attend did so, including Alex and the Stevenses. Reverend Knox appeared. Sadly, his church, so recently completed, was totally destroyed. *Why could God not have spared it?* Alex wondered. Knox gave a quick service before the meeting. Afterward, he appealed to the more affluent people in attendance. He said that God had spoken to them by sending the hurricane. And what had God said? That they needed to give generously to help those in need, as Jesus had taught them. This was a judgment against those who, despite having been blessed with prosperity, had been far too miserly in their charity to those in need. The attendees passed a plate around. Many people, including Thomas Stevens, donated generously.

"Thank you kindly, everyone," said Knox. "I will be publishing a pamphlet describing the hurricane and the devastation. Many other people of means throughout these islands, especially those unaffected by this storm, will be sympathetic and will contribute lest the Lord should so strike their islands as well." He began to read out loud from a handwritten draft of his account. It impressed all. Hamilton felt inspired by the words. *I should write my own account of the hurricane,* he thought. *I'll send it to my father to let him know what I went through and to assure him that I survived it.*

That evening, home in his bedroom, he began to write.

> *Honoured Sir, I take up my pen just to give you an imperfect account of one of the most dreadful Hurricanes that memory or any records whatever can trace, which happened here on the 31st ultimo at night…. Good God! what horror and destruction. Its impossible for me to describe or you to form any idea of it. It seemed as if a total dissolution of nature was taking place. The roaring of the sea and wind, fiery meteors flying about it in the air, the prodigious glare of almost perpetual lightning, the crash of the falling houses, and the ear-piercing shrieks of the distressed, were sufficient to strike astonishment into Angels. A great part of the buildings throughout the Island are levelled to the ground, almost all the rest very much shattered; several persons killed and*

numbers utterly ruined; whole families running about the streets, unknowing where to find a place of shelter; the sick exposed to the keeness of water and air without a bed to lie upon, or a dry covering to their bodies; and our harbours entirely bare. In a word, misery, in all its most hideous shapes, spread over the whole face of the country….

His writing then shifted into a sermon that would have done the good Reverend Knox proud. In the face of a possibly imminent death and the Final Judgment, what would each person feel?

He signed the letter, "With tender affection, Your Son Alex"

He copied the letter, stowed both documents in his pocket and posted the original the next day. As he headed back home, he met Reverend Knox on the way and asked him how the fundraising efforts were going.

"Very well, indeed," said Knox, cheerily.

"I'm glad to hear it. I would donate to it, but…" He shrugged, putting his hands in his pockets.

"Are you still off from work?"

"Yes. Until the ports reopen, and repairs are made to the office, we remain closed."

"I hope that it will be reopened soon."

"As do I, Reverend Knox. I could use the money."

"What will you use it for?"

"I want to go to college somewhere. I don't know, maybe the American mainland. I think it's less expensive there than in Europe. And I'll study to be either a doctor or a lawyer."

Knox smiled. "I'm sure you will someday, young man. We could use a good doctor around here."

Hamilton's lips thinned. He didn't want Knox to know that once he left the islands he wouldn't return if he could help it. He hoped to find a better place than this to live and thrive. He pulled his hands out of his pockets, not noticing the paper that came out as well and fell to the ground.

"Yes, well, I had better return home before they miss me. I'm helping with the cleanup."

"Good for you, Alex. Give Mr. and Mrs. Stevens my regard."

"I will, sir. Your servant, sir!" He touched the tip of his hat in a farewell gesture, which Knox mirrored.

"Go with God, Alex!"

The young man sped off. Hugh watched him go and chuckled. Alex still didn't have a clue about the little surprise he and Cruger had planned for him. He turned to go. Out of the corner of his eye, he spied a piece of paper lying on the ground that he hadn't noticed before. He bent to pick it up. It was in Alex's handwriting and was addressed to his father, James Hamilton. It must be a copy he had made of the letter he had just mailed. It was too late to call out to Alex. He would return the letter to him the next time they met. His eyes, against his inclination to respect Alex's privacy, began to read. It was an account of the hurricane. Despite himself, he continued to read, rivetted, until he had finished the whole thing. Knox was shocked. This was a far better sample of writing than most well-educated grown men could manage. The boy had talent, no doubt. He must publish this, he simply must! Knox showed the letter to the editor of *The Royal Danish American Gazette* and a few other influential people in town. They all shared his opinion on the merits of the letter. Knox resolved that the next time he met up with Hamilton, he would suggest that the boy submit it to be published in the *Gazette*. Nothing else would do.

It was Friday when Knox, heading through town, saw Alex again. He was assisting with the repairs to the office of Kortright & Cruger. Knox had, of course, made a copy of the letter and had kept Alex's copy in his pocket all week on the off chance that he would meet him.

He went up to Alex. "Master Hamilton," he said.

"Dr. Knox! Good day to you, sir."

"Good day."

"As you can see, we are preparing to reopen!" He smiled broadly.

"Glad to hear it. Alex, about that letter you posted Monday…"

"Sir?"

"You dropped a copy of it."

Hamilton's face lit up. "You found it?"

"Yes."

"Wonderful! I would very much like it back."

"I understand. However, I feel I must confess to you. I have read it. I beg your forgiveness for the invasion of your privacy."

Alex waved his hand dismissively. "There was nothing overly personal contained in it."

"Yes, well, I feel it would make an excellent addition to the *Gazette*, if you would allow me to submit it for publication."

"But it's just a letter."

"No, it is not 'just a letter.' It is a masterpiece. Your descriptions are beyond poetic. They tug at the heart. I must confess that I have shown it to others who agree with my assessment of its merits.

Alex chuckled. "I do appreciate the compliments, but... to have it published...?"

"This is exactly the kind of account that will inspire people to donate more to the relief of the victims."

"Perhaps. Let me give it some rumination. I'll let you know for sure."

"You do that, young man." He pulled out the copy of the letter and handed it to Alex.

Publish a letter? Truly? Alex shook his head. He was okay with his poems being published, but who would ever want to read his letters, other than their intended recipients? He laughed.

A week and a half passed, and Alex had actually given the letter little thought. He was still busy with work and with helping restore the Stevens home. One evening, he took a break and happened upon the letter. He reread it, trying to imagine what thoughts could have gone through Knox's head as he had read it. Now, Alex had to admit, he could see it. Alex had gotten a bit preachy at the time. An appeal to one's concern for the destination of their soul after death could drive a person to more charitable acts. Yes, and if he added a passage, perhaps… yes, there, speaking to those affluent people who could afford to part with some small sum or other… Yes, that would be most effective. Perhaps he should publish it, after all. What could be the harm? And it could be anonymous…

The next time he saw Knox, he would tell him to go ahead and publish it. He picked up his pen and added a passage on a separate piece of paper:

> *Art thou so selfish to exult because thy lot is happy in a season of universal woe? … Look around thee and shudder at the view…. See sickness and infirmities exposed to the inclemencies of wind and water! See tender infancy pinched with hunger and hanging on the mothers knee for food! See the unhappy mothers anxiety. Her poverty denies relief, her breast heaves with pangs of maternal pity, her heart is bursting, the tears gush down her cheeks…. Succour the miserable and lay up a treasure in Heaven.*

A few days passed before their paths crossed again. Knox was elated to hear Hamilton agree to the publication. He penned an introduction, and the letter was published in the *Gazette* on October 3,

1772. It created quite a sensation. That a teenager could have written a composition imbued with such eloquence and depth of sentiment boggled the mind. People began to ask questions about the youth, including asking if he needed money. Hugh replied that he was, indeed, and donations started to roll in. Even before this had started, Knox and Cruger had been working together to raise funds to send Alex to the American mainland to attend college. They had appealed to local successful merchants and planters, as well as to Alexander's cousin Ann Lytton Venton, who had inherited some funds from her father's estate. Alex and Cruger had helped her prevent her greedy and cruel husband from seizing those funds. Alex had been reminded of his mother's husband taking her inheritance money. Now that it had been in his power to prevent this from happening to his cousin, he had happily obliged. Knox had spoken with Ann. She agreed that she owed Alex a huge debt and she intended to pay.

The amount they had raised was almost enough now, according to Cruger's calculations. If a little more was needed, the funds coming in from the publication of the letter should more than suffice.

The time for secrets was over. Knox headed for the office of Kortright & Cruger.

Chapter Nineteen: The Farewell

Knox is back, Alex thought. Once again, the reverend nodded at him, then shook Cruger's hand. But they didn't go into the office. They spoke briefly and glanced a few times at Alex. Cruger nodded his head, smiling.

Knox headed toward Alex, followed by Cruger. Alex stood. "Yes, sir?" he said to Cruger.

"We have something to say to you," said Cruger. "Reverend, if you would do the honor?"

"Thank you, Mr. Cruger. Alex, for some time now, we have been secretly collecting a special fund. This has been going on since before the hurricane. We have had some donors who are close to you: Mr. Stevens, Mr. Cruger, and your cousin Mrs. Venton. Now that your account of the storm has been published, even more money has flowed into the fund."

"A special fund?"

"Yes. And there is one person who shall be its recipient."

"Who?" Alex asked, though he was fairly certain that he knew the answer.

"You."

Alex shook his head. "Thank you, but no. Please, sirs, give it to the hurricane victims."

"Thanks to your letter, we have received additional funds for the relief effort and now have enough to cover all their needs," said Cruger.

"You said you started collecting this fund before the storm."

"That's correct," said Cruger. "We feel your talents are being wasted here. You can be so much more than a clerk, my young man. And the only way to reach your full potential is to go to college. And the only way you can do that is to leave these islands."

"We have contacts in New Jersey and New York who can help you settle in and enroll in a suitable school."

By now, the conversation had attracted most of the other employees in the office and they were gathering around Alexander's desk.

"Listen. It's not that I don't want this. I do. It's that I couldn't possibly accept charity—"

"It's not charity," said Mr. Cruger. "You've already done more for me than I can ever repay. I owe you and this is my way of paying you back."

"No. I'm going to work here and save my money until I can—"

"If you do that, you'll be old and grey before you have enough. You're taking the money and you're going to school to make something of yourself whether you like it or not."

Alex laughed. "I must admit, I have always dreamed of this…"

"Then it's settled! We've already booked you passage on the next ship out."

Alex shook his head, incredulous. 'I just can't believe this is happening. This *is* really happening, isn't it?"

Knox nodded. "Oh, it's happening, all right. And no one is more deserving of this than you are."

"Thank you!" Impulsively, Alex hugged the men. "Thank you both! I'll go see Ann and thank her as well!"

"And then you had best get packing," said Cruger.

"I have very little. Just my clothes and my books. What else is there? What do I take with me?"

Knox pointed to an envelope he was holding. "Here is a little money for the trip, your boarding pass, and some letters of introduction to our friends." He handed it to Alex.

"It's been a pleasure working with you, Alex. I will miss you," said Cruger.

"I'll miss you too and all the others." He started to laugh. "I'm going!" His face broke into a bright smile as he looked around at his coworkers. "I'm really going!" His coworkers cheered. They shook his hand and thumped him companionably on the back, giving him words of encouragement and well wishes as he headed for the door.

"It always makes a man feel good to know he's done a good deed," said Knox, smiling proudly.

"You know, Reverend, I think you're right."

Alex thanked his cousin and invited her to come with him, but she declined. "It is not possible at this time for me and my little girl. But perhaps someday… I have always been interested in the continent. God be with you, Alex."

"And you, Ann. I'll never forget you and your generosity to me. If there's ever anything I can do for you, let me know."

"I will."

He kissed and hugged her in farewell.

Alex went home and talked with Mr. and Mrs. Stevens, who were already aware of the situation. They promised to send a note to Mr. McNobeny to excuse Jemmie so he could say goodbye to Alex.

"Give our love to our little Neddy when you see him," said Mr. Stevens. Alex would definitely pay him a visit at Kings College, though he most likely would not enroll there. Reverend Knox had spoken highly of the College of New Jersey in Princeton. "We'll write him a letter and let him know you're coming."

Alex thought for a moment. "No. Let it be a surprise."

Stevens laughed. "Good idea. Oh, if only I could see the expression on his face when you show up out of the blue."

Alex wrote a letter to his father, letting him know what was going on; he would write him again once he was settled and let him know his new address so they could continue to correspond. Then, on the morning of his departure, he had a special goodbye to make.

In the shade of the mahogany trees, he stood before the grave. Grass had grown over it. It had been years since she'd left him. In that time, he had visited here many times when he felt in need of a quiet moment to sort out his feelings. Somehow, he felt like his mother was with him again at these moments, lending him a sympathetic ear as he spoke of his troubles. Adorning the mound was a small, bright-red wildflower in full blown. Alex knelt and picked the flower. It smelled sweet. "I shall keep this forever, to remind me of your sweetness and beauty." He placed it in a small leather bag he had and put it in his pocket. He laid his hands on top of the grave and closed his eyes, connecting spiritually with his mother. After a time, he began to tell her, in French: "I miss you,

Maman. I will do my best to make you proud of me. Please watch over me, Papa, and Jemmie. Please pray for them, for Neddy and the Stevenses, and Cousin Ann and everybody else." He kissed the ground. "Adieu, Maman. Je t'aime pour toujours." *I will love you forever.* When he straightened back up, he realized that tears were streaming down his face. He wiped them away with his handkerchief.

It was almost time. He headed for the harbor and located his ship, *The Waters of St. Croix*. He saw his coworkers, friends, relatives, all of the Stevenses and, of course, Knox and Cruger. He also saw the one person he had hoped would show up more than any other: Jemmie. His brother had grown since Alex had last seen him; Alex imagined Jemmie was thinking the same about him. "You didn't think I'd miss saying goodbye to my brother!" Jemmie said.

"I've missed you."

Jemmie laughed, tears in his eyes. "You're about to miss me a whole lot more, I reckon."

"Come with me."

"I can't. Not now. Maybe, someday."

Alex nodded.

Jemmie handed Alex a bag he was carrying. Alex reached in and pulled out a small portable writing desk. "I made this for you," said Jemmie. "I figured it would come in handy at school."

Hamilton examined the desk admiringly. "It most certainly will. Thank you so much." He hugged him. "I love you, big brother."

"I love you too, little brother."

Thomas Stevens gave him a book bag. "You'll need that for college," he said.

Alex hugged the whole family, thanking them for the present and, especially, for having given him a home when he'd needed one.

"Bon voyage, Alex," said Cruger. "I know you'll do very well. I may be returning to New York someday, so this is not goodbye, just adieu."

"I certainly hope to see you again. And may your business continue to prosper."

"This is for you." He handed Alex a couple of large books that he was somewhat familiar with: Malachy Postlethwayt's *The Universal Dictionary of Trade and Commerce*.

"What, I can keep it?"

Cruger nodded.

Alex hugged him. "Thank you! Thank you so much!" He placed the volumes into the book bag.

Knox handed a wrapped package to Alex. "Another present?"

"Yes."

"It's like it's my birthday!"

Alex opened it. It was a book entitled *Discourses on the Truth of a Revealed Religion and Other Important Subjects* written by Knox himself. "This is wonderful! I'll have something new to read on the trip. Thank you, Reverend Knox!" He hugged him.

"My pleasure, Alex. Enjoy it. And mind you pray every day and read your Bible. And… if you would, don't forget your old friend Dr. Reverend Hugh Knox."

"I won't. I'll write you. May God bless you and keep you."

"You, too, Alex. You, too." There were tears in Knox's eyes.

"Oh! I almost forgot." Alex reached into his jacket pocket and pulled out a manuscript. "I wrote this poem and thought you might want to have it published in the *Gazette*. It's inspired by my favorite poet, Alexander Pope."

"If it's written by you, I'm sure it's more than good enough for publication."

"All aboard!" a ship's crewman called out.

"That's my cue," said Alex. "Goodbye, everybody! Thank you! God bless you all!" He started to walk, waving at everyone. They waved back. After a few minutes, the ship's sails were unfurled and caught the breeze. The ship started to slide away from the harbor. Alex kept watching until he could no longer see the people.

He thought of the poem he had given Reverend Knox, *The Soul Ascending Into Bliss.* It spoke of one who had died and was going to Heaven. Indeed, Alex was saying goodbye to the life he had lived thus far. His departure was a kind of death. He would never again see most of the people he had known in the islands. All the sights, smells, and sounds of the West Indies would be gone, replaced by strange ones. He would meet new people, and hopefully befriend many of them. The poem encapsulated much of his feelings at the time, especially the first two lines:

AH! whither, whither, am I flown,
A wandering guest in worlds unknown?
What is that I see and hear?
What heav'nly music fills mine ear?

Etherial glories shine around;
More than Arabias sweets abound.
Hark! hark! a voice from yonder sky,
Methinks I hear my Saviour cry,
Come gentle spirit come away,
Come to thy Lord without delay;
For thee the gates of bliss unbar'd
Thy constant virtue to reward.
I come oh Lord! I mount, I fly,
On rapid wings I cleave the sky;
Stretch out thine arm and aid my flight;

For oh! I long to gain that height,
Where all celestial beings sing
Eternal praises to their King.
O Lamb of God! thrice gracious Lord
Now, now I feel how true thy word;
Translated to this happy place,
This blessed vision of thy face;
My soul shall all thy steps attend
In songs of triumph without end.

For now, his destination would not be Heaven; he would encounter new challenges and opportunities, all of which was exactly what he needed. He had never been so excited in his life. Alexander Hamilton strode proudly to the bow of the ship and looked ahead. His future was there. It would be a great one; he would make sure of that.

Appendix: Why I Wrote It What I Wrote

In January of 2019, I started listening to the Original Broadway Cast recording of Lin-Manuel Miranda's *Hamilton: An American Musical.* The play was being performed locally at the time and tickets had all but sold out. What was the big deal? I wondered. I was soon to find out. From the very first words: "How does a bastard, orphan, son of a whore," I was intrigued. Hamilton's mother was a *whore?* How did that work? Did she… um… *service* her clients while little Alex was off in a little bedroom somewhere trying to read a book? I started to research Hamilton's life and shortly was to discover that much of what has been said about him, both in the musical and in books, is simply untrue, most especially the part about his mother being a prostitute. I discovered that Rachael Faucette's ex-husband had accused her of "whoring with everyone" in his divorce complaint (certainly an untrue claim) and that, years later, James Callender had written that she was a camp girl (i.e. a prostitute who services soldiers in a military camp). Nothing could be further from the truth, although, admittedly, Rachael had committed adultery. Why she had done so (because her husband abused her), and with how many men (two), I was later to discover.

As I was researching Hamilton, I started to strongly feel an urge to write a book about him. Not just a biography, though I have written a brief one of those. But a novelized, more readable, account of his life. Partly, this was inspired by other attempts at the same. Although the others have been well-written, I have been, to some degree, at least a little disappointed with every single one of them for various reasons. Some of them contain factual inaccuracies. Some are told from his wife Eliza's point of view when most of the real action is with Hamilton himself. Some don't provide enough detail. Not a single one of them has an explicit love scene depicting the details of Hamilton's wedding night. If they weren't going to write it, I decided that I would do it (wait for book 3).

Soon after starting to write, I realized that this would be a huge undertaking that could not be contained within one book. I decided to divide the story into separate volumes, of which this book is the first part.

It took me about a year to research and write this book. In December of 2019 and at other times in 2020, I posted first drafts of bits from all the volumes on my Facebook and Instagram profiles and quickly acquired fans who clamored for more. I wanted to write parts 1-3 (1 being this book, 2 being Hamilton's life as a college student and 3 being his life during the Revolutionary War) and then publish them as the first volume. I still intend to do this, once they are all three written, which may take another year or two. Part of the problem is that there is still much research to do, especially involving the Revolutionary War, and writing a story good enough for publication takes numerous revisions which takes *time,* and lots of it. I am not a historian, nor am I a professional writer. I have a full-time job, a family, a house, and some hobbies, all of which take up most of my time. But, still, I desperately wanted to write these books and publish them.

Fast forward to March of 2020. The coronavirus was invading the United States, bringing with it the deadly COVID-19 illness. I have multiple "underlying conditions" and am in my fifties. I was greatly concerned about my survivability should I catch the virus before a vaccine could be developed. The more I heard, the more likely it seemed that I would catch it and die. Since then, I have been fortunate enough to be able to work remotely from home. It is my intention that at least this part may be published. Will I finish any other part? I certainly hope so, but nothing in life is guaranteed, including the continuation of life itself. All of the above reasons tell you why I am publishing part 1 as a standalone book.

What (hopefully) lies ahead? The following is a listing of all of the parts. This is subject to change as I progress in the writing:

Book Two – The Collegian

Book Three – The Hero

Book Four – The Statesman

Book Five – The Framer

Book Six – The Secretary

Book Seven – The Discontented

Book Eight – The General

Book Nine – The Sacrifice

A note on the use of language:

I have written most of the dialogue of this book in a 21st century style. Alexander

Hamilton's style of writing is quite different from my own. I certainly can imitate him if I choose to, and occasionally give him dialogue which sounds more like himself. I will continue to do this at times. I have decided not to take direct quotes from things he has written, as others have done, because when I read a direct quote it jars me a little because he *wrote* that and if he ever expressed the same sentiments out loud, he most likely would have done so with slight alterations in phrasing.

For the most part, I choose to write in my own style as it is more enjoyable and readable for a modern-day audience. On those few occasions in which we have transcripts or word-for-word accounts of what he actually said, his word choice was sometimes simpler than his writing style, sometimes not. In future parts of the story, I will, on occasion, put in a few words commonly used in the 18th century which are now archaic, to give it more of an air of authenticity. In the correspondence of Alexander Hamilton, he wrote "'tis," "'twas" or "'twill." I tried to write his dialogue in that manner, but it "sounded" too weird, so I stuck with the modern parlance instead.

I have endeavored through exhaustive research to present you with as accurate a verbal portrait of the real Alexander Hamilton. You may question the manner in which I filled in some of the gaps in our knowledge of his life in the islands. If so, please read my responses to the questions below. I feel justified in my choices. Much to the frustration of myself and a multitude of biographers, little is actually known of Hamilton's life while living on the islands in the Caribbean. Some of what you can read in laudably well-researched books such as Ron Chernow's *Alexander Hamilton* and Michael E. Newton's *Alexander Hamilton: The Formative Years* is theory and conjecture as well, so I feel it is my right to do the same. Below are the main speculations I have made.

Question #1: Why did Rachael leave her son Peter?

This was one of the questions about Hamilton's early life and, in particular, about his mother, that bedeviled me. Hamilton wrote very little about his mother, but according to his grandson Allan McLane Hamilton, Alexander's sons said that when Alexander spoke of his mother, he did so with a considerable degree of affection*.

Therefore, she must have been a kind and loving mother to him and her other children with James. If that is true, how could such a good mother have left her first-born son? There must have been something that motivated her to do so. I was inspired to write a scene, after her release from prison, where Levine tried to subjugate her in an embarrassing and sexual manner right in front of their son. The only plausible explanation I could come up with that made sense was that Rachael concluded her son would be a better man without witnessing continual spousal abuse, especially of a sexual nature.

*James Flexner (in *The Young Hamilton: A Biography)* did not have the imagination sufficient to explain this contradiction so he claimed that Hamilton's sons were lying, and that Hamilton hated his mother. I strongly disagree with him.

Question #2: Why did you have Rachael and James get married without her first getting divorced from Levine?

On August 26, 1800, Alexander Hamilton wrote a letter to William Jackson in which he wrote that after his mother left her husband, she "went to St. Kitts, became acquainted with my father and **a marriage between them ensued** [emphasis mine], followed by many years cohabitation and several children. But unluckily it turned out that the divorce was not absolute but qualified, and thence the second marriage was not lawful." [Source: founders.archives.gov] The fact that Hamilton mentions a marriage at all indicates that it is most likely that his parents had an actual marriage ceremony in a church which they may have kept secret because of its unlawfulness. No record has ever been found of this wedding, so either it was not recorded, or the record was lost. In that time and place, if a couple who were both single lived together for a sufficiently lengthy period of time as husband and wife, they were considered to have a common law marriage. However, James and Rachael could not make this claim as only one of them was actually single. Obviously,

Alexander could only have known about the marriage because his parents had told him. I find it hard to believe that they would have lied to him. They would have shared with him the court's ruling on his mother's divorce which did not free her to re-marry, thereby rendering her marriage to James null and void.

Question #3: What year was Alexander Hamilton born?

One of the most debated and controversial issues surrounding Alexander Hamilton was the year of his birth. From the time he moved to the American mainland, and throughout the rest of his life, Hamilton claimed he was born on January 11, 1757. Unfortunately, there is no record of Hamilton's birth, no birth certificate, not even a record of his baptism (assuming he had one). For many years, everyone accepted that 1757 was his year of birth. It was called into question by the discovery of the probate court's record of his mother's estate, which, in 1768, stated that Alexander was 13 years old, therefore born in 1755. A few other, though disputable, records from the islands, also supported this contention. In *Alexander Hamilton: The*

Formative Years, Michael E. Newton argued very persuasively in favor of 1757 being the correct year, tearing apart and disputing the accuracy or reliability of the documents which supported the 1755 theory. I will not repeat his arguments here (I recommend highly that you read his books), other than to say that the documents of that place and time were notoriously unreliable in their accuracy. Newton, however, reversed his opinion on the matter in his subsequent book *Discovering Hamilton…* on the basis of one document: the court record that included the testimony of Rachael Levine's sister Jemima Gurley at the Levine divorce hearing in April of 1759. Gurley stated that 2 years before she had visited her sister on the island of St. Eustatius, where Rachael had had two children, aged 5 and 3, and that their father was not John Levine but a man Rachael was living with. Therefore, assuming that Alexander was the three-year-old, he couldn't possibly have been born in 1757, but rather in 1754 or 1755. But was this the case? Gurley did not state the names or even the genders of the two children. One can easily assume that she was referring to James and Alexander, given that – according to the probate record - they and Peter Levine were the only children that outlived her. However, it is quite possible that there may have been at least one other Hamilton child, a child who predeceased his or her parents. In fact, Chernow presents this theory in his book in part to explain what inspired Hamilton to write a very emotionally-charged eulogistic poem after the death of Anna Maria Boudinot, the little girl of friends of his (I will cover this poem in part 2). It is clear that Rachael Levine was a fertile woman, having had her first child about a year after getting married to John Levine and her second about a year after moving in with James Hamilton. Most of her siblings (some of whom, probably, were half-siblings) died very young. Only three children of Rachael's father Jean Faucette survived into adulthood. The West Indian islands were particularly plagued with infant mortality from various diseases. It's almost a foregone conclusion that Rachael and James had more children than James, Jr. and Alexander. The child of theirs who was five years old in 1757 could very well have been someone *other* than James, Jr. Taking in consideration the arguments Newton presented in his first Hamilton book, is it not possible that Hamilton was, in fact, born in 1757 after all?

Furthermore, let us consider the following. (1) He was reported to appear to be younger than his stated age. I can buy that maybe Hamilton had a baby face. And some have said he was short. By 21st century standards, a 5'7" man is below average in height. But people were shorter on average in the 18th century and 5'7" was the average height of a man. Contemporaries who knew him said he was of "middling" height, not short. He was, at one point during the war, described as a "mere stripling." If Hamilton had been born in 1754 or 1755, this "mere stripling" (i.e. a boy) would have been a fully grown 22 or 23-year-old. Hardly a stripling, nor too short to be considered a boy. It's less likely that people would have said he looked young for his age if he was actually 2 or 3 years older than he was claiming to be. (2) Hamilton was notoriously honest and candid. He could have spread lies about his political opponents and benefitted from such, as Jefferson and his cronies such as James Callender did about Hamilton in various publications of the time. But he didn't. When James Reynolds was extorting huge sums of money from him by threatening to tell Hamilton's wife about the adulterous affair he was having with Mrs. Reynolds, Hamilton could have spared the expense and lied to his wife, saying there was no affair. But he didn't. Why would such an honest person lie about his age? Chernow and others have theorized that it was to make himself appear closer in age to the other students at college. I doubt that was the case, knowing Hamilton's character as I do. Hamilton wasn't the kind of person who would conform to others and make himself more popular by telling lies. He preferred the truth. As he wrote in "A Full Vindication…" (see part two for more) "'Tis my maxim to let the plain naked truth speak for itself…." Therefore, it is my belief that the plain, naked truth of the matter is that Rachael was pregnant with Alexander when her sister visited her late in 1756 or early in 1757 to help her move to Nevis and that he was subsequently born on January 11, 1757, as he said he was. This book shows how the time and place of Hamilton's birth was as he said it was and still in accordance with the testimony of Jemima Gurley. She didn't mention in court that Rachael had been pregnant at the time of her visit. Levine's counsel didn't ask her if her sister were pregnant; they didn't need to. They had already proven that Rachael was living with a man other than her husband and had had children by him.

The bottom line is, absent any indisputable record of Hamilton's birth, there is no proof that he lied about the year of his birth. I, for one, believe him, not some court which had possibly made faulty assumptions about the boys' ages. I rest my case. Next question.

Question #4: Why did you make Alexander's other sibling a girl and name her "Marie?"

Statistically, it's likely Rachael had a girl at some point, not just boys. What would she have named her? It was typical at that time to name children after oneself or a close relative, such as a parent or sibling. Rachael, therefore, likely would have named her daughter after her mother Mary but may also have wanted to honor her French father and gave her the French variant of the name: Marie. Also, I find it interesting that (as I discovered after writing about the daughter with this name) that the Boudinot's daughter was named Anna Maria, but in the poem, Hamilton referred to her as "Maria" not "Anna." Could the similarity between Anna's middle name and Marie's name have inspired Hamilton to write the poem – and especially to write it from the *grieving mother's* point-of-view - recalling the memory of witnessing his own mother mourning her lost daughter? It seems quite plausible to me.

Question #5: Why does this book contain mature material?

Why not? (1) No other Hamilton book has it. (2) I want to read it but, other than fan fiction, no one else is writing it, so I guess I have to. I'm not a big fan of censorship in general (except, of course, for anything involving minors). Think of the popularity of sexually explicit romance novels. Or of the horribly written *Fifty Shades of Grey* series. Most people want sex in their lives. It's only natural, and I see nothing wrong with depictions of sex between two consenting adults. Without it, none of us would exist. I will admit, however, that I understand that some people are offended by it and/or that they would like their children to be able to read about Alexander Hamilton, but would prefer they not read this book because of its mature content. At first, I thought about all the other books about Hamilton that contain little or no mature content. People can just read those instead. But then I thought I might like children and offended adults to read my books after all. Therefore, I decided to edit the book into a "clean" edition and publish that as well. Naturally, I much prefer the uncensored version for my own personal reading. The only real qualm I have had is that I wrote about Alexander's first forays into the world of sex when he was 13 and 14 years old. I did censor myself to some degree even in this edition, for, as I've stated, I agree with censorship when the material involves minors. I must point out, however, that in the 18th century, it was acceptable for a girl to get married at the age of fifteen. Hamilton's mother, it is believed, was married at sixteen. In my book, Sally is fifteen and Coelia sixteen when they get involved with Hamilton. Nevertheless, I understand how people may find these things objectionable and I share that sentiment. Therefore, I purposely wrote very implicitly as it concerned his sexual interactions with the two girls.

"But then, why even put Hamilton's early sex life in there at all?" you may ask. Several reasons. First of all, I am setting the stage for Hamilton's extensive sexual proclivities which will come to full fruition later in life. Secondly, I am convinced, as are others, that a physically attractive and precocious young Hamilton, infused with the urges of a young, teenaged boy and without parents around to closely monitor his whereabouts and activities, lost his virginity – or at very least, made his first "excursions in the flowery walks, and roseate bowers of Cupid" - on the island of St. Croix. (For example, Robert Hendrickson wrote in *Hamilton I (1757-1789):* "the novelist Gertrude Atherton's powerful intuition told her that Kitty [Livingston] 'was the first to reveal to him the fascination of her sex,' however much or little that cryptic phrase may mean, if less than all. However, it is unlikely…. It would be ridiculous to assume that a handsome teen-ager growing up in the tropics… would spend every waking hour ambitiously preparing for futurity and war…. to a greater extent than any other framer or founder… Hamilton seemed to excite the hopes and fears aroused by what later times might call the image of the sensuous man.") Thirdly, he wrote two erotic poems in 1771, at the age of 14, and must have had some experiences with at least two (very different) girls by that time to inspire the writing of said poems. Fourthly, it's a known fact that Hamilton, as a grown man, had quite a few sexual partners, especially during the Revolutionary War. Even after marrying his beloved and ideal life-mate Elizabeth Schuyler, he had sexual intercourse with *at least* one other woman (Maria Reynolds) and flirted - possibly more

- with many others. Rumormonger James Callender (although at times a not-so-reliable source of information) and other, more honest people, wrote of Hamilton's reputation for being a ladies' man. In response to this and other allegations, Hamilton wrote the Reynolds pamphlet in which he acknowledged that he did have a reputation but, other than admitting to his adulterous affair with Maria Reynolds, he did not confirm or deny the validity of said reputation. If the rumors were false, why didn't he just outright deny them? I will say far more on this matter in a future book. In fact, I may someday write a book that deals exclusively with the Reynolds affair itself.

As for the rape scene, I had to explain why Rachael left Levine. Physical abuse was bad enough, but once it turned sexual, and she had a place to escape to, she left him. As for the attempted rape of Alex, it simply came to me. It was far more dramatic than anything I had had in mind before to explain how he had made the acquaintance of Thomas Stevens and his son Edward. It is a fact that a lot of criminals were transported to the West Indies as well as Australia, and that some of them would have been rapists. Sadly, some were transported merely for the "crime" of being homosexual. It's not at all outside the realm of possibility that at least one of them was a rapist who may (or may not) have also been a homosexual and may have found Alex walking alone one evening and attempted to sexually assault him. I apologize to anyone who is offended by this, as I am not homophobic in the least and most certainly do not mean to suggest that rapists are more common in the LGBTQ+ population than among heterosexuals. However, it is a sad fact that rapists exist in all demographics.

Question #6: Why did James Hamilton, Sr. leave his family?

There is no extant letter from James Hamilton, Sr. that explains why he left his family. There is no record of Alexander ever explaining why it happened. According to the most plausible conjecture on the subject, and the written evidence that supports it, it must have been for the reasons stated in the letter I've composed for the text of this book. The fact that James was a financial wreck is written on more than one occasion by Alexander Hamilton in various letters he wrote. Alexander continued to correspond with his father and vice versa and both wrote affectionately to and about each other, which indicates that lack of love – at least between the father and his sons - was not a motivation for the separation. Alexander invited his father (and brother James) to his wedding (they were unable to come) and invited them to move to America to be closer to him. Neither was able to make the move. On June 12, 1793, James wrote to his famous son:

> *Dear Alexander*
>
> *I wrote you a letter in June 1792 inclosed in one to Mr. Donald of Virginia Since which I have had no further accounts from you. My bad State of health has prevented my going to Sea at this time being afflicted with a complication of disorders.*
>
> *The war which has lately broke out between France & England makes it very dengerous going to Sea at this time, however we daily expect news of a peace & when that takes place provided it is not too late in the Season I will embark in the first Vessel that Sails for Philadelphia.*
>
> *I have now Settled all my business in this part of the World, with the assistance of my good freind Mr. Donald who has been of every Service to me that lay in his power in*

contributing to make my life Easy, at this advanced period of life. The bearer of this, Capt. Sherref of the Brig, Dispatch Sails direct for Philadelphia & has promised to deliver you this letter with his own hands, & as he returns to this Island from Philadelphia I beg you will drop me a few lines letting me know how you & your family keeps your health as I am uneasy at not having heard from you for some time past.

I beg my respectfull Compliments to Mrs. Hamilton & your Children, & wishing you health & happiness, I remain, with esteem

Your very Affectte. Father

James Hamilton

[Source: founders.archives.gov]

I think it is obvious that James didn't distance himself from Alexander out of any lack of love. I do not think that James questioned the paternity of his children, as some historians have suggested since he obviously acknowledged in the above letter that he was Alexander's father. I do not think he left out of fear that he and/or Rachael would be arrested for adultery since, legally, she was no longer married to Levine when they moved to St. Croix in

1765. I think the separation was prompted by his financial misfortune and also out of love for Rachael, giving her the chance to find someone else who could be a better provider. Also, the separation gave Rachael's rich relatives an excuse to help support her (which they did initially) and their children since she no longer had a man-of-the-house who had that responsibility.

Question #7: Did Alexander Hamilton actually meet his half-brother Peter Levine?

It's possible. They were both in Christiansted at the same time when Peter returned there to claim his inheritance in 1769. It's not hard to imagine that Peter would have had a certain degree of curiosity about his half-brothers, particularly the one whose work for Nicholas Cruger may have already gained him some notoriety at that time. Peter also would have wanted to speak with him about what it was like to grow up being raised by the mother he had barely known before she left him. Initially, I thought of writing about the meeting and decided not to. I didn't know what explanation to give as to why Peter took all of the inheritance money and didn't split it with his half-brothers. Then, inspiration hit me again after having done a little research. Peter had been a successful merchant in Beaufort, SC. He may have had an opportunity to expand his business and needed the money. In addition, he, no doubt, partially supported his impoverished father (just as Hamilton would support his own later in life). He saw that his half-brothers were being well provided for so he may not have felt guilty about taking the entire inheritance, especially since it was not a large sum. The Stevenses were rich and successful enough to support another child, especially one who had a job and was bringing in some income as well. It is also interesting to note that upon his death, Peter Levine left a small amount of money to his half-brothers. Perhaps he was motivated to do so after having met one of them or perhaps he felt he owed them that much. My main impetus for writing the scene was that I felt it was important to wrap up the loose ends of the Levine story and to show that Rachael's wish for Peter to turn out different from his father had come true. I also wanted to show the sad but deserved conclusion of John Michael Levine's life – after the death of his second wife and their children, Levine died alone and penniless in 1771 in the hospital in

Fredericksted, St. Croix, where he had worked as a janitor.

Bibliography

The main sources of information for this book (though by no means the only ones – in fact, I've read just about every book on Alexander Hamilton that you can name) are listed below.

Alexander Hamilton by Ron Chernow

Alexander Hamilton: The Formative Years and *Discovering Hamilton…* by Michael E. Newton

Alexander Hamilton volume 1: Youth to Maturity 1755-1788 by Broadus Mitchell

The Intimate Life of Alexander Hamilton… by Allan McLane Hamilton

The Papers of Alexander Hamilton volume 1

founders.archives.gov – an extensive online archive of many works written by the founding fathers.

For more information on the terrible treatment of slaves in the 18th century Caribbean, I highly recommend:

Sugar in the Blood by Andrea Stuart – an excellent book about slavery and the growing and processing of sugar cane in the West Indies

Note:

The sermon delivered by Reverend Hugh Knox contained his actual words, which I edited and condensed from multiple passages in his book *Discourses on the Truth of Revealed Religion and Other Important Subjects*

Acknowledgments:

I would like to thank Lin-Manuel Miranda, whose brilliant musical (which I have seen performed live and in person on multiple occasions, as well as the recorded film on Disney+) inspired me to learn more about Alexander Hamilton and led to this book being written. I owe him far more than I am willing to state publicly.

I would like to thank the many authors whose books I have read, too many to mention, but here are the main ones: Ron Chernow, Michael E. Newton, Broadus Mitchell, Allan McLane Hamilton, Robert Hendrickson, John Church Hamilton, Gertrude Atherton, Willard Sterne Randall, Richard Brookhiser, Forrest McDonald, Paul Collins, Stephanie Dray, Laura Kamoie, Richard Sylla, Henry Jones Ford, William G. Chrystal, Arthur S. Lefkowitz, Philip Thomas Tucker, and Thomas Fleming.

A special thank-you goes out to Harold C. Syrett, Jacob E. Cooke, and many others who contributed to editing - and researching the very valuable footnotes of - the massive 27-volume set of *The Papers of Alexander Hamilton*. Although the set is now out of print and expensive and difficult to collect (I have a few volumes that

I found online for a decent price), its documents are fortunately available for free on founders.archives.gov. Many thanks also go out to anyone involved with the online project.

Above all, thank you, Alexander Hamilton. For everything. And I mean *everything.*

Diane K. McCarty, 2020

About the Author

Diane K. McCarty was born in Milwaukee, Wisconsin and was raised in Hamilton County, Ohio. She has written published biographies and short stories. She works for the government. She can be found online on Facebook: Diane ThePhoenix Awen and Instagram: @dianethephoenixawen

The following is a preview of *Passion: The Life and Loves of Alexander Hamilton, Book Two: The Collegian*

Passion: The Life and Loves of Alexander Hamilton

Book Two: The Collegian

Chapter One: The Journey

Alexander stood at the bow of the ship, staring intently at the open sea ahead of him. His mind filled with dreams of the glorious future he would have. This idyllic reverie was rudely interrupted by the gruff voice of a sailor yelling at him.

"Hey, kid!"

Alex turned as the man approached him. His weather-worn clothing had been repaired multiple times, its colors faded by much exposure to the sun. His tanned, leathery face was full of wrinkles. The whiskers on his chin were partly grizzled. Despite his age, his arms were well-muscled.

"Ye'll want ta stow yer gear below."

"What?" Alex looked down to where his trunks sat at his feet. "Oh, yes."

"Dere should be an open berth down thar somewheres," the crewman said, scratching his chin thoughtfully. "Grab one before dey're all taken."

"Thank you, sir."

The man barked a laugh. "Ye don't need ta call me 'sir.' I ain't no officer; just a reg'lar sailor."

"Oh. Sorry, sir. I mean—"

"Ye ever been out ta sea before, kid?"

"Not the open sea like this. Just short trips between the islands."

"Well, get used ta dis view. Ye'll be seein' it fer weeks. At least, ye better hope this is all ye'll see. We dinna want ta get caught in no bad storm."

Alex nodded and turned green at the thought. The motion of the sea was starting to get to him. He heaved and tasted vomit in his mouth. "Excuse m—" He leaned over the railing and threw up.

To Alex's chagrin, the seaman laughed again. "Dinna worry, lad. Ye'll be fine once ye get yer sea legs and kin keep some food doon." He threw a flask at Alex. The youth caught it with ill grace, took a swig and almost coughed as he recognized the taste: rum. He swallowed with difficulty and the liquor burned his throat.

"Ye got a name, kid?"

"Alexander Hamilton, at your service, s—" Hamilton choked out, his throat raw.

"Samuel Jones at yers," the man replied, bowing with mock courtesy.

Alex smiled. "Pleased to make your acquaintance."

"Ye need some help carrying yer things?"

"No, I think I can manage."

"Good. Because I have duties to tend ta and I've already wasted enough time on ye. The captain'll string me arse up if'n I dinna hop to it." Even though his words were somewhat rude, he spoke with a friendly tone of voice that let Alex know the sailor wasn't angry at him. "See ya 'round, kid." He slapped Alex on the shoulder so firmly that it nearly knocked him down. The man stepped away with a roguish smile on his face, chuckling softly.